THE HERALD
DIARY

THE HERALD DIARY

Another Stoater

Ken Smith

BLACK & WHITE PUBLISHING

First published 2014
by Black & White Publishing Ltd
29 Ocean Drive, Edinburgh EH6 6JL

1 3 5 7 9 10 8 6 4 2   14 15 16 17

ISBN: 978 1 84502 812 1

A CIP catalogue record for this book is available from the British Library.

Typeset by Iolaire Typesetting, Newtonmore
Printed and bound by Gutenberg Press, Malta

Contents

Introduction

What a year for Scotland!

First, the Commonwealth Games beamed pictures of happy smiling Scots around the world. Then the independence referendum showed half the population smiling and the other half glum. So, what are we Scots going to talk about now?

Well, one of the things readers of *The Herald* newspaper talked about was all the daft and funny things that happened to them during the year – and then sent the stories to *The Herald*'s 'Diary' column for everyone else to enjoy.

Here are the best of them.

1

Glasgow

No matter how difficult life becomes, Glaswegians will often shrug their shoulders and remark: 'Ah well, you've got to laugh.' Here are a few of the things they were laughing about.

JOHN MARLETTA spotted a chap in a full red metal outfit, dressed as film superhero Iron Man in Glasgow's Buchanan Street, where people were slipping him a bob or two to have their picture taken with him.

Two police officers went over for a chat, no doubt checking whether he had a street entertainment licence. John says: 'Iron Man was very sheepish and docile with the police to the extent that a passer-by said to him: "Not so hard now are ye?"'

A READER was dining in a popular Italian restaurant in Glasgow when the young woman at the next table asked for pepper on her penne pasta. After the waiter had returned with the grinder, used it over the dish and walked away, the woman muttered to her friend: 'At what point do you think that Italian waiters stopped trusting Glaswegians with the pepper?'

PEOPLE can be a tad harsh at times. A reader in Glasgow heard two women discuss a friend who was struggling keeping her weight under control. 'She's had her stomach stapled,' one confided. 'Stapled to what?' asked her pal. 'Greggs?'

AMERICAN comedian Dave Fulton, compering a show of American stand-ups at the Glasgow Comedy Festival, loves coming to Scotland. But he admitted: 'I was on Bath Street when I asked a local for directions. After he starting talking to me, my eyes drifted down to his stomach in the hope that subtitles would appear there.'

GLASGOW International Comedy Festival reminded those attending to make sure they switch off their mobile phones. We recall the comedy gig where the no-nonsense comedian, fed-up with an audience member's phone ringing, grabbed the phone and answered it himself with: 'Hi, I don't know whose phone this is – I've just picked it up by a car crash.'

ANDY CUMMING tells us about the chap who worked in a Glasgow south-side taxi office, and always drank Jim Beam American whiskey in the pub afterwards. The taxi drivers nicknamed him 'The Despatcher on The Rye.'

FOLK were posting their strange stories about Glasgow on the social media site *Reddit*, with one local reminiscing: 'Saw a guy get punched unconscious in the middle of the road outside a nightclub. Everyone piled around him, wondering what to do, when some lassie breaks through the crowd, saying, 'Let us through, ah know furst aid, let us through'. She kneels down next to him, unloosening his laces saying, 'Ye awright pal, ye awright, aye just stay still', and then runs off with his shoes.'

THE storm down south reminds David McKenzie of Glasgow's great storm of 1968 when his parents lived in the west-end. David says: 'At three in the morning, slates were crashing from the roof. A neighbour decided to see if his new car was safe. Due to the wind, his wife persuaded him to dig out his old air raid warden tin hat from the war and wear it for protection.

'The inspection of the car showed it was parked in a sheltered spot, and no damage had occurred. Satisfied, he started to return to his flat when a gust of wind caught the edge of his tin hat, removed it from his head, and sent it straight through the windscreen of his new car.'

WHAT'S been happening in the Maryhill area of Glasgow, you might ask? Hector MacAllister tells us: 'Over the last five months contractors have been installing new lamp posts in Garrioch Road and other nearby streets. The job has yet to be completed as the old lamp posts still have to be removed.

'Last month new litter bins were installed along the length of Garrioch Road. Guess which lamp posts they were attached to?'

THE May Day celebrations in Glasgow ended with a cabaret in Òran Mór as the organisers wanted the workers' celebrations to expand from just being an annual march and rally. The main turn at the cabaret was subversive comic Mark Thomas who handed out sticky round labels such as you see on books. Thomas's versions read either: 'Also available in Charity Shops' or 'Staff Recommendation: Keep the Receipt'. He suggested folk surreptitiously put them on books by Tony Blair and Jeremy Clarkson when they are in a book shop.

MANY will sympathise with stand-up Eleanor Morton at the Òran Mór show who mused: 'Have you ever come home from a day out where you did not meet a single friend, not even a work colleague or even a neighbour, and you sat there thinking to yourself . . . I can wear this outfit again tomorrow?'

AN article about tenement life in *The Herald* reminded older readers of having to share a toilet on the landing with other families. One chap, born and raised in Springburn, argued there was one good thing about the shared toilet. When his friends asked what that could have been, he replied: 'You seldom got a cold seat.'

WE mentioned 'First World Problems' and a south-side reader tells us: 'I once heard a woman moan that she had to keep moving around her house in order to avoid her cleaner.'

RHYMING slang has always featured in the Glaswegian vocabulary including 'Joe the Toff ' for 'I'm off' when someone leaves.

Recalls Kevin Toner: 'I was with some mates in The Horse Shoe Bar and in the company of some folks up from Dorset.

'Later on, one of our local guys stood up and said, 'Right, I'm Joe the Toff, nice meeting you all' and walked out of the bar. Cue questions from our southern friends about how this Joe got to be known as 'The Toff'.

A RECENT innovation in Glasgow parks is folk taking disposable barbecues with them on sunny days. It became so popular that the parks folk put a large plastic bin in Kelvingrove Park for the disposal of said barbecues. Sadly it was burned to the ground.

A new metal bin has now replaced it, with the sign carrying the additional information that they should be extinguished before being deposited.

THE news Robert Burns' original handwritten 'Ye Banks and Braes o' Bonnie Doon' is to be sold by Bonhams for an estimated £30–40,000 reminds us somehow of the Burns Supper speaker who called in at Govan library to brush up on Burns' verse before he spoke. 'Robert Burns – the complete works,' he told the librarian when he strolled in.

'The massage parlour is next door, Mr Burns,' she replied.

OUT of nowhere we are sent a Glasgow joke. It reads: 'A Glaswegian bangs on his neighbour's door and tells him: 'Do something about your dog. It's been barking for hours and I've got a terrible hangover and need some sleep'.

'You shouldn't have crawled into his kennel then,' replied the neighbour.

A NEWS story revealed that the 'Scottish Hair and Beauty Awards' being held at the Thistle Hotel in Glasgow ended in a bit of a stramash with ball-gowned women fighting and baring their bums. As one reader asks: 'Glasgow hairdressers? Do you think anyone shouted out 'Tongs Ya Bass'?'

EVERYONE in Glasgow is pleased that the much-loved School of Art has been saved, although the damage inside is appalling. However, one reader watching the rescue of the burned artefacts on the TV news tells us: 'Seeing someone carry out a still smoking piece of wood, I couldn't stop myself from wondering if it was next year's winning Turner Prize.'

GLASGOW International Comedy festival has announced a 'Watch With Baby' comedy show when parents can go out on a Sunday afternoon to see adult comedians without the expense of getting babysitters for their weans.

Jojo Sutherland, who is compering the gig at Òran Mór, declared: 'It won't be the first Glasgow audience I've played to that's made up of people crying, shouting and vomiting.'

GOING to the vet is becoming increasingly complicated with the wide variety of tests now available. One Glasgow south-side dog owner was told by the vet that he wanted to carry out a test on his pooch's liver function. 'No need to worry,' the owner replied. 'I've banned him from strong drink for a while now.'

SCOTS comedian Stu Who, discussing faux pas, told of some young ladies at a gig at Glasgow's People's Palace who asked for a lift to Cumbernauld in the van. Stu agreed, as long they helped load the gear.

Says Stu: 'One of the ladies, a petite thing on high heels, passed me holding one tiny box in one hand, and her handbag slung over the other arm. 'What's wrong wae you?' I inquired. 'Only got the one arm?'

'She put down the box of records, and her handbag, and with a pop, removed an artificial arm, which she thrust into my hands.'

DON'T you just love it when Glaswegians try to be a little bit posh? A reader tells us about her south-side cousin who saw a rat in the basement of her large house and called in help from the council's environmental services. After he laid some poison down, he was asked by the householder: 'Is it efficacious?' As the chap was not old enough to remember the old Scaffold hit *Lily the Pink*, he looked puzzled. So our reader stepped in to help: 'She means does it work?' 'Work?' he replied. 'It'll blow their bloody semmits aff.'

THE website Glasgow Guide has been discussing whether begging should be made illegal on the city's streets. One member told them: 'I once saw a bloke outside Greggs in Partick holding a sign saying, 'Haven't eaten in four days'. As I was going into Greggs for a chicken and mushroom slice I thought I'd get two and give the guy one of them.

'I handed the bag with the slice to the beggar and walked away. The next thing I know I got hit on the back of the head by the chicken and mushroom slice and heard the beggar cursing at me. Since then I have ignored all beggars.'

JANETTE from *The Krankies* still seems to be hurting after her accident, when she fell from the beanstalk while appearing in pantomime at the Glasgow Pavilion. This year she is at the SECC in *Dick McWhittington*. At one point she told the audience: 'Oh, I could do with a sleep. I wonder what's on at the Pavilion?' Unfair Janette. Surely it's behind you?

MIKE RITCHIE was at Celtic Music Radio's Clutha benefit gig in Glasgow where a player of the clairseach – the Celtic harp – told him of being on a late-night train home where a friendly drunk, spotting his instrument, encouraged him to play a tune. Reluctantly, and to keep the peace, he began removing the harp from its case. The inebriated traveller got to his feet and declared: 'Quiet, please. The harpoonist's gonnae gie us a tune.'

LOTS of bedraggled old Christmas trees are lying on the streets of Glasgow waiting to be collected. A reader tells us: 'I regularly pass an embankment on the new M74 extension in Glasgow where I noticed that a few fir trees that had been planted there had disappeared in the run-up to Christmas.

'But good old Glasgow: they've now been returned over the fence – dead.'

A READER who was out for a meal in Glasgow heard the young lady at the next table, obviously not a fan of an entire glass of ice, ask the waiter: 'Diet Coke please – but with very little ice.'

There was clearly a bit of a misunderstanding as the waiter came back with an ice cube on a spoon and said: 'We don't have any ice cubes smaller than this.'

A SOUTH-SIDE reader tells us she told her husband that she was going to cook pak choi for dinner. He replied that he didn't know what that was, so she held it up to show him.

In a typical Glasgow way he told her with a hint of disappointment: 'It sounded so fancy too. Yet, at the end of the day it's just something green.'

A READER swears he heard a chap in a Glasgow pub announce to his pals: 'I tell girls I'm on performance-related pay.'

'It sounds better than saying I'm a busker in Buchanan Street.'

OH yes it is . . . panto time has arrived in Glasgow. Stars from the King's Theatre's *Aladdin*, Karen Dunbar as the Slave of the Ring and *Still Game*'s Gavin Mitchell as the evil Abanazar, were in full costume on the platform of St Enoch's Subway station to have their picture taken for a special promotion which gives Subway ticket holders money off their panto tickets.

As they posed for the photographer a train arrived and a chap getting off took in the scene and asked them: 'Has your magic carpet broken doon?' before walking past.

A SOUTH-SIDE dog owner walked into his golf club at the weekend and trumpeted: 'Some big munter barged into me in the park earlier. She was wearing a pink t-shirt, with 'Birthday Girl' emblazoned across the chest. She asked, "What do you think I'm going to turn today?"

"Milk," I replied.'

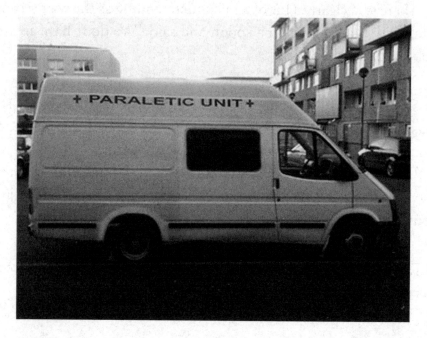

A READER who attended Scottish Opera's wonderful production of *Don Giovanni* at Glasgow's Theatre Royal tells us: 'During the interval I visited the Gents which on that particular floor are very small and quite cramped. I took my place in the short queue and waited patiently. When the chap in front's turn came, he suddenly announced in a loud theatrical voice, 'I'm sure it's shrunk since I was here last'.

"I take it you mean the room?" I asked. He quickly replied "Yes" with a bit of a red face.'

OUR tall tale of the escaped lion from the former Calderpark Zoo prompts a reader to tell us: 'I was in Easterhouse at the time, and two police officers came running towards me shouting that a lion had escaped.

"Which way is it headed?" I asked.

"Are you daft?" one of them replied. "You don't think we're chasing it do you?"'

MOST folk begging on the streets of Glasgow are poor souls sitting placidly on the pavement. But occasionally at night you meet a more aggressive drunk looking for cash. One reader heading home after a night out was approached by a slightly swaying chap looking for money. Patting his change pocket, our reader amicably told him: 'Sorry pal, I don't have a washer.'

'Do I look like a plumber?' the chap replied.

THE west end of Glasgow can be home to the occasional luvvy. A reader swears he was in a diner there when a chap leaned over to the next table and asked the customer sitting there: 'Are you—?' Before he could finish, the diner loudly replied: 'Yes, I'm in the touring production at the Theatre Royal this week.'

The confused chap who started the conversation told him: 'No, I was only going to ask, are you finished with the ketchup?'

GLASWEGIANS are always keen to help visitors to the city. On a sunny Saturday a chap on Dumbarton Road in Partick was stopped by an English tourist, who asked him: 'Are you familiar with this area?' Trying to be honest with her, he replied: 'Only if you're looking for a pub.'

She hurried on instead after thanking him.

GLASGOW'S George Square has reopened after being cordoned off for a facelift before the Commonwealth Games. Crossing the square, James Lland heard a local opine: 'I can see the real losers in the rumpus over the square being closed off – the pigeons are looking gey scrawny!'

GLASGOW waitresses. Bruce Henderson from Maybole says: 'Back in the fifties, when Reo Stakis forayed into French cuisine with his Cadoro Bistro in Glasgow's Union Street, my wife and I paid a visit. We ordered Creme de Pompador for starters and as the waitress unceremoniously kicked open the swing door into the kitchen, she shouted, 'Two toma'a soups.'

BAND names. Jim Buchan says: 'A numpty friend was flicking through the Glasgow gig guide and commented that The Scotia was featuring a band called 'TBA' at the end of the month.

'He then piped up: "Ye know that band must be good, as they get plenty of gigs around the city. They're playing loads of pubs."'

A READER ponders on the reassurance given by a ned in Glasgow who had a menacing-looking dog with him. He told a woman who stopped to pet the animal: 'Don't worry, hen. She only bites folk I set her on.'

2
Commonwealth Games

Glasgow, not the city with the fittest citizens it has to be said, warmly welcomed the Commonwealth Games – despite the traffic problems – and dived into the events faster than Tom Daley. Here are some of their highlights.

OLYMPIC champion Jessica Ennis-Hill will miss the Commonwealth Games in Glasgow because she is pregnant. John Park in Motherwell is disappointed. As he tells us: 'She pulled out despite organisers' assurances that she'd look right at home in Glasgow as a pregnant woman in a tracksuit.'

WRITER Hardeep Singh Kohli has been writing about his native Glasgow in the latest British Airways *High Life* magazine. Looking forward to the Commonwealth Games, he confidently stated: 'We are destined to have an unforgettable summer.'

He must have felt the need to qualify that, however, for those who are not used to the city. He added: 'I use the term 'summer' more as a calendar reference than any indication of balmy/sun-soaked/blue sky meteorology.'

THE sports website *Inside the Games* has been warning that there may be many empty seats at the opening and closing ceremonies of the Commonwealth Games in Glasgow due to the high cost of the tickets (up to £250). It quotes one local who showed that indomitable Glasgow spirit by declaring: 'Bought two opening ceremony tickets. Think I may have a seat next to Sir Chris Hoy, given what I paid for them.'

'GREAT start for Scotland in the Commonwealth Games,' muses reader Bill Smith, 'anybody notice that Scotland's first two gold medals were for fighting? And the participants were from Coatbridge? And they were wimmin?'

VOLUNTEER drivers have begun shuffling officials and dignitaries around for the Commonwealth Games, with distance being no object. A reader tells us about her volunteer sister who suggested that the delegate she was chauffeuring could visit some of the highlights of Glasgow and the surrounding area. 'What about going to see Ben Lomond?' she asked.

'Who's he?' replied the delegate.

YES, Glaswegians are determined to give a good welcome to Games visitors. *Still Game* actor Gavin Mitchell tells us: 'Met a nice wee happy guy in Tesco who told me, 'Aye ah'm across the road in the pub there wi' some English people – ye know The Games innat. Never tried tablet. Tablet! Imagine that! Cannae huv that. Poor souls.' He produced his shopping bag full of it, winked and staggered into the traffic back towards the pub.'

GOOD to see that 'Clyde', the Games mascot, has already won an award. The satirical American television show *Last Week Tonight* described Clyde as 'winner of the creepiest mascot on earth' competition. So maybe not the prize the organisers were hoping for.

Incidentally, the show tried to explain the Commonwealth Games to Americans by stating: 'A once mighty nation gathering together the nations it lost, and finding a way to lose to them once more.'

THE Queen's Baton for the Commonwealth Games had a successful tour through Ayrshire at the weekend. Among the cheering crowds in New Cumnock was one local who, observing the entourage that went with the Baton, commented: 'We hivnae hud so many polis in the village since the Miners' strike.'

Incidentally, one police motorcyclist with the baton was asked if they had volunteered for the job. 'Aye, you could say that,' he replied, 'but, in reality, we were voluntelt.'

FINALLY, after wandering all over Scotland, the Queen's Baton arrived in Glasgow for the Games. Reader Patricia Cox tells us: 'As the baton passed by in one area of Glasgow some of the locals were less than impressed about the speed of the baton bearer. One said: "If I had that many police vehicles chasing me I'd be a lot quicker than that."'

THE tartan outfits, reminiscent of Brigadoon, have been unveiled for the Scottish team to wear at the opening ceremony of the Commonwealth Games. Not everyone is charmed by them, with one critic comparing them to Loganair stewardesses from the sixties.

Perhaps harshest was the Twitter user who stated: 'I wonder if the designer was at the Glasgow School of Art and the fire there was a desperate attempt to stop it going forward.'

ONE of the stars of the opening ceremony was being stopped in the street and being mobbed by fans. No, not crooner John Barrowman, but Jock, one of the terriers that led in the teams with such gallus style. People were stopping, wanting their pictures taken with him. Jock's owner, Jacqui, says the dogs were well looked after, even with folk on hand to spray them with water if they were getting too hot. It was only at the dress rehearsal that one of the other dogs got a bit excited and did on the stage what dogs do naturally. It led to the director shouting into the ear-pieces of the performers: 'Watch out for the turd! Watch out for the turd!' At least we think that's what he was referring to, and certainly not opening singer John Barrowman . . .

WE liked John Quigley's reaction when Sir Chris Hoy, dining in John's Red Onion restaurant in Glasgow city centre, came to the aid of a fellow diner. Said John: 'What a gent, as you would imagine. Lady at table next to him left her bag, and he sprinted down Bath Street to reunite her with it.

'Dipped it first mind you. Joking!' And for you foodies out there who want to know these things. Sir Chris had scallops and monkfish – and loved it apparently.

JOHN McNAB of Troon was on a packed train heading to Glasgow when an African visitor, talking to an elderly Glasgow gentleman, expressed disappointment that the weather had deteriorated when it was so sunny at the start of the Commonwealth Games.

'Ah, but we're into August now – this is the rainy season,' the Glasgow chap explained. When the tourist asked how long the rainy season lasted in Glasgow, the chap replied: 'till the end of July.'

SOME flash gear the athletes have these days at the Games. It reminds Sheriff James Murphy of different times when his brother was head gym teacher at a school in Stirling. Recalls James: 'There was no tradition of athletics at the school, and my brother, himself an athlete, tried to introduce it. To encourage his more enthusiastic lads, he took a small party to the Scottish Schools Championships in Edinburgh. Of course they won nothing, but were not downhearted. As they explained on the bus home, "Sir, we had nae chance. They hud nails in their saunies."'

SARAH SILLARS in Malmesbury, Wiltshire, tells us her mum was going through security at the Games when the security chap asked her if she had any smart phones or tablets in her possession. 'No, I'm not on any medication,' she replied.

OVER at Hampden, comedy writer and actor Sanjeev Kohli was taking in the athletics. 'I refuse to join in,' he tells us, 'the sarcastic hand-clapping for the high jumpers. How can that possibly be helpful?'

IT'S not just the spectators and stewards who have been on great behaviour at the Games. John Sheridan in Airdrie tells us: 'I was strolling down the street outside the West End Bar when the Guyana cycle team passed. The last rider tailed off and came up to join me on the pavement and asked if I could open a litter bin next to me. He then deposited a small piece of paper with the words, "Such a pretty town. Would not want to drop litter". I was well impressed.'

Shame on you, dear reader, if your first reaction is to think 'Airdrie?'

THE outbreak of illness at the athletes' village reminds retired teacher Moira Campbell: 'My favourite sick note from a parent stated that her son was absent due to 'direrear' – in my opinion a very apt description of the effect the ailment has.'

TALKING of Twitter, a spoof account for Stansted Airport posted: 'Lots of tracksuits on flights to the Commonwealth Games. We can't tell the difference between athletes and the Glaswegian brides and grooms.'

SATURDAY was a particularly hot day, and signalling failures meant many of the crowded trains taking folk to Games destinations were running late. Joy Murray was on one such train when a passenger asked the ticket seller if the heating was on.

'Och yes', was the reply, 'it's because the windies are all open. It's boiling isn't it?'

LONG queues for buses out to Hampden from the park and ride, which made a few folk unhappy. But throughout the city there have been bands of enthusiastic volunteers helping visitors get to their destinations. Says one south-side resident: 'As I approached Central

Station for my train, I was confronted by two eager youngsters clad in their volunteer kit, asking politely if I need directions to anywhere. 'Er . . . not really. I live here,' I reply. They look crestfallen, so I allowed them to point me towards Platform 15.'

WE mentioned the BBC captioning the south-side park as Bella Houston. Inevitably it encourages readers to remind us of the classic – very old, that is – tale of the woman at Glasgow Queen Street station asking at the ticket office: 'Maryhill, single.' So the chap behind her put his cash down and said: 'Alex Smith. Married.'

ONE of the many successes of the Games has been the entertainment zone at Glasgow Green, though the need to have bags checked by security does lead to queues. One family of tourists were queuing the other day when the wee boy in the party told his mother that he could put his head through the metal fence they were standing beside. Immediately the wee Glasgow wumman in front of them turned round and chided him: 'Don't you dare. Your mammy disnae need that on a day like this.' Suitably chastened, the wee lad behaved himself.

AND still the visitors stream in to Glasgow. Anne Paterson tells us: 'You hear all sorts of accents when crossing from Queen Street Station to George Square. I heard a mother with push-chair and several small children announce, "Now Rory, if you are going to get hysterical, we'll just turn round and get back on the train to Edinburgh."'

AFTER a gold medal winner failed a drugs test at the Games, Stephen Grant commented, a tad harshly: 'You can't ban athletes at the Games for having traces of drugs on them. They've been walking around Glasgow for a fortnight.'

THERE have been big crowds using Mount Florida station after the athletics at Hampden. The platform was crowded the other night as the flow of trains to Glasgow Central was interrupted by a train going the other way to Neilston. Many visitors were unsure where Neilston was, and a chap with a loud voice declared: 'Been to Neilston a few times.'

Then he added: 'Mind you, that's only because I've fallen asleep on the train.'

A FINAL story of the Games audiences, and Linda Brown tells us of the vocal encouragement at the para-powerlifting. Linda says: 'A lifter from the tiny Pacific island of Nauru was being spurred on by one of the team who was shouting out to her various instructions to win, in, presumably, Nauruan. Not to be left out, a Glaswegian who could not speak Nauruan but wanted to encourage an overseas guest shouted out in encouragement, 'What she said!'

FAREWELL then to the great Commonwealth Games in Glasgow, but we will long remember the Clydesiders – the cheery volunteers – who helped make it a special occasion. As Mike Ritchie says: 'As we made our way to the SECC Precinct, with my eight-year-old giving high-fives to every Clydesider possible, one of them, spotting a glum-faced gent, shouted out cheekily, 'You're no in Edinburgh noo – go on, smile.' And the bloke did.

IN fact we only had one report of a Clydesider not being appreciated. A reader tell us: 'One Clydesider at the entrance to the Games Village in Dalmarnock was pleased to enthusiastically welcome four well-dressed newcomers. On completing his green foam-finger waving and well-rehearsed pleasantries, one of the four, a sinister-looking man in a black suit, put our humble volunteer in his place. "That is no way to address the Vice-President of Uganda!" he barked.'

A FINAL tale from the entertainment zone at Glasgow Green. One of the barmen was making tidying up a bit easier for himself by offering a few bob to kids to collect discarded drinking cups. One youngster got carried away and went up to a drinker still quaffing his beer and asked: 'Are you finished with that?' The man was heard saying: 'That's the first time I've been told to drink up by an eight-year-old.'

BEWARE the immediacy of modern technology. BBC Scotland online reporter Jamie Ross was at the Games wrestling, and tweeted: 'They're zooming in on audience members and forcing them to dance. So afraid. This is why I don't leave the house.'

Minutes later a worried Jamie tweeted: 'Oh my God! The

commentator just read my 'This is why I don't leave the house' tweet out loud, and then tried to identify me. I might have to leave.'

WE mentioned the BBC captioning the south-side park Bella Houston during the Marathon. It reminds Nancy Brown in Kilmarnock: 'Many years ago when the evangelist Billy Graham was speaking at the Kelvin Hall there was a story going around that his wife was not happy as she had heard that he was spending too much time between Bella Houston and Maryhill.'

THE Commonwealth Games have not been forgotten. Roy Cameron was on the train from Glasgow to Balloch when the ticket inspector came through from the end carriage. Immediately three teenage lads leapt to their feet and ran into the next carriage. Roy says: 'The ticket examiner exclaimed, "I thought Usain Bolt was away hame!"'

REMEMBER Commonwealth Games President Prince Imran struggling to get the top off the Queen's Baton in front of millions? Well, the Prince was later seen in Glasgow's Mussel Inn, accompanied by about thirty of the Malaysian team, where he was tucking into a lobster bisque.

Staff were gobsmacked when he struggled to get the pepper grinder to work – and someone had to quietly point out he was holding it upside down.

AND a final tale from a Games volunteer with Donald Macdonald telling us: 'I was lucky enough to cycle with Tucker Murphy, one of the Bermudan tri-athletes – on condition it was a recreational cycle. When we first met up to plan a route it was one of the really hot days and I complained it was too hot and he replied, "This isn't hot."'

'On the day of the cycle there was some drizzle and he complained about the rain, to which I could only reply, "This isn't rain."'

ALREADY the Commonwealth Games seem a fading memory. As Robert Bennie tells us: 'I believe I may be suffering from Post Games Syndrome. Everyone has stopped smiling at me, it's pouring with rain, the papers have nothing to write about, I have completely lost my feel-good factor, the football season has started, and I can't find a polis anywhere!'

3

Pubs

Some of the funniest and most astute conversations take place in pubs. Mind you a lot of rubbish is talked there as well. Hopefully we have brought you more of the former rather than the latter.

A GLASGOW reader swears to us he was in a bar in Finnieston when the peace and quiet was shattered by a gaggle of women arriving and demanding drink after attending a Michael Bublé concert in the nearby Hydro arena. They all wanted served at once so the under-pressure barman shouted out: 'Right, let's do this the easy way. Oldest first.'

Suddenly, says our reader, you could have heard a pin drop.

WE asked for your bar staff stories, and Robert White in Kirkcudbright says: 'In a famous horseshoe-shaped Glasgow bar, I asked for a bowl of soup. When it arrived there was no roll, so I asked for one. The barman rolled his eyes and said, "You're pushing the boat oot noo." He lifted the last roll in the bar, tore it in two and gave me a half. "I need that other bit for my soup," he said.'

UNDERAGE drinking. Terrible thing, of course, now that it is years since we did it. But as Andy Cumming recalls: 'One friend who wanted his illegal first pint had some immature moustache hair on his top lip, so he decided to fill it out with his sister's eye-liner to make him look older. The first pint was great. But after he sported a rather fetching gringo Mexican-style of facial hair.'

'I SAW a guy drop litter,' said the bloke in a Glasgow pub. 'I like my city, so I just picked it up and didn't say anything to him.'
  'What was it?' asked his pal. 'A tenner,' he replied.

WE mentioned underage drinking, and Eric Duncan in Cardross recalls: 'A friend was in a pub in Glasgow's Barmulloch when he was fifteen. Under the suspicious stare of the barman, his mate coolly asked for a pint of heavy. My friend, however, for some reason not wanting to emulate his pal, scrabbled around in his head for a grown-up drink, eventually settling for a Pimm's No.6 that he'd once seen in his aunt's drinks cabinet in a more salubrious part of the city.
  'Needless to say, this sad lack of forward planning led to a quick termination of the bevvy session.'

WE end our yarns on wine with Stuart Russell reminding us of a classic tale: 'My first boss told the story about being out for dinner in the Central Hotel. The wine was off and the waiter was summoned and told the wine was corked. After a moment's pondering he replied, "Aw the best wines is corked, sir."'

WE asked for your memories of the robust dances at the Highlanders' Institute in Glasgow, and Sheila Campbell in Argyll tells us: 'Many years ago, I was at the Highlanders' when an Islay chap was dancing too enthusiastically and fell heavily. He was bleeding quite badly, so was persuaded to go to the Western, and a couple of hours later, we were surprised to see him back.

'My friend worked at the Western and looked at his medical notes which recorded that he had been more concerned about the loss of the half-bottle in his pocket, than the fact he needed eight stitches in his backside.'

JAMES Martin tells us about a woman who admits she can't remember large chunks of her evening after drinking too much wine with friends. She calls it 'Sauvignon Blank'.

BAR staff continued. Moyra Peffer tells us: 'An American on holiday in Glasgow was out for a meal with friends at an upmarket restaurant in the Merchant City.

'Enjoying their coffees and liqueurs, the waitress appeared at the table, unannounced, with the bill, her coat on, and with the request, "Gonnae pay yer bill, so I can catch the last bus home, pal?"'

A READER in a Glasgow pub heard a young chap further up the bar who was sipping a soft drink decline the offer of a pint with the remark: 'I'm allergic to alcohol.'

As this surprised the folk with him, he added the explanation: 'Whenever I take it I break out in handcuffs.'

OUR pub pies stories remind Martin McGeehan: 'In Greenock, we tell of the barman who suggests today's special offer to the customer. 'A pie, a pint and a kiss from the barmaid – £4,' he says, and nods towards his female assistant.

'The customer looks at the barmaid for a few moments and asks, "Is it an Aulds pie?"'

FRUIT and veg, it seems, are still strangers to many a Scot. An Ayrshire reader tells us his teenage grandson came home from his shift in an upmarket local restaurant and, when asked how his day went, he replied: 'Terrible. I had to try to explain to a diner what cauliflower was.'

BERT Peattie in Kirkcaldy recalls: 'My favourite dish in my local was sausage, beans and chips. It was well known that I preferred my beans cold. One day after placing my order, I noticed that people who had ordered after me had been served, while I was still waiting. I caught the barmaid's eye, and she dashed into the kitchen, reappearing with my dish. "Sorry Bert," she apologised, "we were blawn oan yer beans."'

A CHAP in a Glasgow bar the other night was discussing the state of his finances when he came out with the memorable explanation: 'Whenever I feel spontaneous, my bank account quickly reminds me to calm down.'

A STIRLING reader, just back from a holiday in Spain, was much taken with the sign on the wall of the pub he frequented, which stated in English: 'Bars are one of the few places that will solve your problems – and create your problems at the same time.'

GERRY MacKENZIE was in a Yoker pub when a purple-faced, slightly worse-for-wear gentleman exploded through the door and lurched to the bar. Gerry says: '"A hauf and a hauf pint a' heavy, please," the man managed. The charge-hand poured the drinks, and the customer slammed a fistful of very small change down and picked up the whisky and downed it in one. He had started on his half pint as the charge-hand had finished counting the smash. "Here", said the barman, "there's only sixty-eight pence here."

"That'll be aboot right," said the toper as he put down the empty beer glass.'

STUART TAIT continues our underage drinking stories with: 'On starting at Glasgow School of Art, one of my new friends, a fresh-faced seventeen-year-old James Macleod from Skye, said he wanted to go and try a pint in a Glasgow pub. So with grant cheque in hand – remember them? – we headed to a bar on Holland Street where James, on being asked what he would like, said "Beer" to which the barmaid asked, "What kind?" His reply of "A big one, please!" abruptly ended that particular bevvy session.'

BAR staff continued. Andy Cameron tells us that the late great Glen Daly was once served a whisky with ice in it, and when he complained that he didn't ask for ice, the Glasgow barman replied: 'It's only ice – it'll no' dae ye any harm.'

'Tell that tae the captain o' the *Titanic*,' replied Glen.

'HAD some barbecue-flavoured crisps at the weekend,' said the chap in the Glasgow pub.

'Didn't like them,' he continued. 'Tasted of grease-covered metal and charcoal.'

A READER was in a Glasgow pub at the weekend when a fellow toper declared: 'I always follow government advice to pull to the side of the road if you are tired and have a nap.'

'Mind you,' he added, 'my passengers never seem happy about it.'

WE read the news story that the makers of the bams' dram, Buckfast, will be bringing out a version of the fortified wine in cans rather than glass bottles – safety campaigners say it will mean fewer drunken bottle attacks.

Anyway, it reminds us of when the prestigious *New York Times* had a reporter in Coatbridge writing about Buckfast and he gave a flavour of the Lanarkshire town by putting in print: '"It goes straight to your head," said passer-by Martin Rooney, forty-eight, "but it's not my cup of tea" (Mr Rooney noted that his cup of tea is half a bottle of vodka a night).'

WE asked about underage drinking and Colin Campbell recalls: 'I celebrated my eighteenth birthday in the Riverside Inn in Callander. Confused bar staff, on noticing the rather large '18 today' badge on my t-shirt, observed that I'd been drinking in there for about a year.'

A COUPLE of young chaps in a Glasgow pub the other night were discussing a mutual friend who was apparently putting on a bit of weight. Eventually one of them declared: 'I'm not saying he's greedy, but he probably cleans the inside of his cooker with a slice of bread.'

AS we call time on our underage drinking stories, Gordon Hay in Livingston tells us he was DJ-ing at the age of sixteen in Inverness, when he started going afterwards to the Haugh Bar where he was made welcome as they were a man short for the domino team.

Says Gordon: 'After a few weeks as a regular, however, I was embarrassed when my Dad, who had got wind of where I was, arrived to howk me out. I remember him berating the barman for serving me and hearing the barman's plaintiff reply that they needed me for the dominoes that night.'

PUB conversations continued. Dougie McNicol was in his local in Bridge of Weir when a friend was talking about an acquaintance who works at Glasgow Airport. 'She's got a great job,' he said. 'She started out as an air hostess and got quite high up.'

'Well she would, wouldn't she?' remarked a chap further up the bar.

BOUNCY, chirpy radio announcers – you either love them or hate them. Paul Cortopassi tells us of a radio interview where the person being questioned was asked at the end 'Do you like *10cc?*' so that the presenter could segue smoothly into the next piece of music. 'I'm more of a quarter-gill man myself' was the classic reply.

BAR STAFF continued. Andy Cameron dusts off the yarn of American actor David Hasselhoff going into a Glasgow bar while he was in the city, judging the auditions for *Britain's Got Talent* a few years ago. When the barman asked: 'What can I get you, Mr Hasselhoff?' the American entertainer cheerily replied: 'You can just call me The Hoff.'

'OK,' said the barman. 'Nae hassel.'

JOCK LAIDLAW in Lockerbie recalls on underage drinking: 'Still at school, we used to chance our arms in the local hostelry.

On one occasion, having ordered a few pints, we were asked by the barmaid to confirm we were indeed eighteen, as she was aware that the police were doing the rounds. At that, one of our number thinking on his feet said 'Well, better make it a half-pint then.'

WE ended our underage drinking stories, but somehow we forgot to mention students. Harry Shaw in Airdrie recalls: 'In the sixties, Charities Week included an inter-uni drinking competition.

'Our man from Strathclyde Uni could down a pint in 2.3 seconds and a yard of ale in under 8 seconds.

'When he won the competition, a tabloid newspaper came to do an article on him, but he insisted that they didn't take his picture, as he was only seventeen and he didn't want his mammy to know what he had been up to.'

WE asked for your bar staff stories and naturally we were reminded about the Glasgow barman who, when asked for a slice of lemon in a gin and tonic, replied that they weren't a branch of Malcolm Campbell's.

In a similar vein, Brian Logan recalls: 'In the seventies, I took a friend to a Glasgow pub where he ordered pie, beans and chips.

'When he asked the barman for brown sauce, the reply was, "What do you think this is? The Ritz?"'

WE asked for your underage drinking tales and Jen Hogg, now in Netherlee, recalls: 'I remember one trip to the pub in St Andrews aged sixteen or so.

'Some of us came in from the outlying villages, and it was rather unfortunate that the bus driver who had brought my friend in, turned up in the pub, spotted her with a half of snake-bite-and-black in hand and shouted across the crowded bar at her: "You paid a half!"'

HIGHLANDERS' Institute continued. Kate Woods lived near the HI in Berkley Street, and at chucking-out time often heard the drunken strains of the 'Northern Lights of Old Aberdeen', or some-such. Kate says: 'One evening we heard a window yanked up and a very irate Glaswegian yell, "If youse teuchters wanny see the Northern Lights, I'll boot yer erses there the noo – nae charge!" There was silence for a moment, and then the singing resumed. We decided that the singers were Gaelic speakers and had not yet learned the finer points of the Glasgow dialect.'

OUR mention of the robust dancing at the Highlanders' Institute in Glasgow reminds Paul O'Sullivan: 'My parents used to go to a ceilidh in Glasgow on a Saturday evening. At that time, dances had to finish before midnight on a Saturday to avoid people having fun on the Sabbath.

'Every Saturday half a dozen big Heilan' cops used to turn up at the ceilidh about 11.30 pm.

'They would check out the dance and all the conditions very seriously, then they would take off their caps and dance reels till five to midnight when they would put their caps back on and tell the band to stop playing.'

A READER in a pub in Dundee heard a visitor, not enamoured of the city, ask a local: 'Can you tell me one thing Dundee is famous for?' He felt the reply 'Piece of cake' was genius.

GOOD to see Helen Mirren being given a Fellowship from Bafta. We remember when Helen was in Glasgow filming *Heavenly Pursuits* in the City Chambers. She and some of the crew dropped into the Press Bar where she asked what wine they had. Bearing in mind this was thirty years ago, the reply was 'red or white.'

She opted for white, took a sip, and with all her actorly skills kept a smile on her face while she discreetly pushed the glass further up the bar.

OUR story about Dame Helen Mirren's limited wine options in Glasgow reminds Ronald Oliver in Elie: 'I was at an architects' do in Glasgow City Chambers, and as the meal was a sit-down nosh with wine, we were asked by the wine waitress: "rid or clear?"'

AS SCOTLAND drags itself back to work after the New Year, a woman in Renfrewshire is heard complaining to friends: 'I think that Scotland is awash with toxic lemons – every time I have a drink with lemon, I'm ill the next day.'

THE story of Helen Mirren being offered 'red or white' when asked for wine varieties in Scotland some years ago reminds Bryce Johnston: 'There was the guy who went into the chip shop in Troon and was asked if he wanted sauce. "Aye, tomato sauce, please," he said.
'To which the girl replied: "Sorry, we've only got rid or broon."'

'I NEVER make the same mistake twice,' the chap in the Glasgow pub opined the other night. As his pals looked impressed he added: 'I usually make it six or seven times before I'm convinced.'

OUR tale of the chap who wondered if the paddle steamer *Waverley* was so named because people waved from it, reminds a reader that a lack of knowledge of Scottish history is not uncommon. He said: 'Two men were having a drink in the James Watt bar in Greenock when one asked if the place was named after the boxer. "Don't be silly," said his pal, "it was named after the college."'

THE full moon in Scotland just now has been captivating. As Ally Buchanan tells us: 'I was walking back from the local pub last night, with the full moon shining hazily through the clouds. One of the lads I was with gazed up and said: "I wish I could paint that." The other lad replied, "You'll need a long brush."'

DISCUSSION at a Glasgow pub the other night got round to the lottery with one regular claiming: 'I'm going to use the numbers from my gas meter reading for my lottery ticket. It seems to work for Scottish Gas.'

4

New Technology

Some folk still find new technology, smart phones, and social media baffling. Others, mainly the young it has to be said, have taken to it like ducks to water. Here are their stories.

YES, many parents happily now text their children, which is not always appreciated. One Glasgow teenager showed us a text from his mother in reply to one of his which contained the usual abbreviations. Texted his mother in reply: 'It's before, not b4. I speak English, not bingo.'

GRAND THEFT AUTO V, the latest computer game sensation, was developed in Scotland, which is why references to Scotland are always sneaked in. This time Hawick is a drug-infested area in the game.

We also like the fact that the fake stock exchange, based on the American Nasdaq, is given the more Scottish version, Bawsaq.

DO younger people spend too much time using technology, asks a reader? He heard a girl in the Botanic Gardens tell her pal: 'Did you see how funny that puppy was? It was like watching a real-life YouTube video.'

INTERNET dating continues to be popular but not everyone is convinced. A chap in a Glasgow pub was encouraged to try it by a friend who told him: '"And this particular site chooses people who share the same interests as you."

"I don't think," replied his pal, "that I would want to date anyone that weird."'

PRICE gougers British Gas foolishly took to Twitter to answer questions from customers about its shocking price rises. Amongst the questions for which its really had no answers, were: 'Which items of furniture do you, in your humble opinion, think people should burn first this winter?' and the more macabre: 'What is the best temperature to thaw an elderly relative at and what seasoning would you use with one?'

TEENAGERS can be so cruel. As one was heard telling his pal on a train into Glasgow: 'My mum's trying to use Twitter these days. It's like watching the raptors in *Jurassic Park* trying to figure out how to open the doors.'

A SHAWLANDS reader realised he was getting old when he told his whingeing young son he sounded 'like a broken record,' and his son asked: 'What's that?'

GOOD to see how new technology can make some of our older traditions easier to handle. Glasgow comedian Frankie Boyle tweeted Des Clarke, appearing in *Aladdin* at Glasgow's King's Theatre: 'We're in the stalls. If you could throw the sweeties quite far, I'd appreciate it.'

A READER waiting for a train at Hyndland station heard a student-type look at his beeping phone and then tell his pal: 'That's my mother sending me a text. I'll give it five minutes then she'll phone me to see if I got it.'

A COMMENT many a parent might have sympathy for – a colleague tells us: 'One of my kids texted 'plz' because it's shorter than 'please'. I texted back 'no' because it's shorter than 'yes.''

COPING with new technology, continued. A reader swears to us that her neighbour told her: 'My daughter texted me saying 'Call me ASAP' but I think I'll just stick to calling her Fiona.'

WE wonder how many readers will identify with Michele Catalano who explained: 'There are two types of people in my life. People who understand that I hate talking on the phone, and my mother.'

FACEBOOK has seamlessly entered many people's lives. Dave Jones tells us that he heard one young chap discussing a mutual friend with a pal and explaining: 'Twenty-one days is a mint jail sentence. He'll be well pleased.' The pal looked at his smart phone and replied: 'Yeah, he's already got eleven likes for it.'

A READER catching a train on the south-side into Glasgow city centre heard a young girl excitedly tell her pal: 'There was a guy in the waiting room, not texting or looking at his phone or anything! Just waiting. Really freaked me out.'

DO we believe the reader who tells us: 'My wife told me the butter in the fridge was rock hard, and could I help spread it. So I went on to Facebook and told everyone that our butter was rock hard.

'Apparently that's not what she meant.'

A CHAP in a Glasgow pub at the weekend announced to his pals that he had downloaded the Lockwatch app on his mobile phone, which discreetly takes a picture of anyone who tries to use the phone and types in the wrong password.

'I've now got eight pictures of me when I'm drunk,' he added.

A POINT about today's world from Rhys James who tells us: 'People will trust you to hold their baby – but not their iPad.'

'I'M getting old,' a *Herald* reader remarked to his teenage daughters the other day. 'When I was young, I managed to go for months without taking a picture of anything.'

A SOUTH-SIDE reader had to phone a financial services company as the form he was filling out online insisted that he put in a mobile phone number – even though he doesn't have one. When he explained to the helpline person that he threw his mobile phone in the sea the day he retired, there was a pause before the company representative replied: 'I wish I could throw my mobile in the sea.'

FAVOURITE Facebook posting we saw yesterday: 'I will be posting telepathically today.

'So if you think of something funny, that was me.'

CONSPIRACY theories abound on the Internet. A Glasgow reader tells us: 'Whenever I see anyone on Facebook or Twitter coming up with some daft theory, I usually contact them to mess with their heads by telling them: "Your conspiracy theories were planted by the Government to distract you from the real conspiracies."'

A COLLEAGUE wanders over and tells us: 'I may be cynical, but I doubt people on social networks are 'laughing out loud' half as much as they claim to be.'

FOR those of you still getting to grips with Twitter, Ian Power tells us: 'I was explaining Twitter to my seventy-four-year-old mum. I said there's lots of joking and showing off. She said, "That's what pubs are for." She has a point.'

JOKES are regularly updated to express how technology is changing our lives. As a reader said yesterday: 'I was stopped by the police driving home from the pub the other night.

"Do you know why I was following you?" one of the officers asked me.

"Because my tweets are funny?" I asked hopefully.'

LISTENING to music has changed so much in recent years, what with folk listening to tracks on shuffle on their iPods. As one reader told us yesterday: 'My friends were discussing when they had last listened to an album in its entirety. One of them replied, "The last time TalkTalk put me on hold."'

COMEDIAN Ben Verth in Edinburgh swears to us – and who are we to doubt him? – that he saw a neddish looking young man at a supermarket checkout in the capital being asked by the automatic self-service machine: 'Have you swiped your Nectar card?' and the young man defensively replying out loud: 'Naw, I got it legally.'

A NUMBER of organisations are tentatively attempting to communicate using the social website Twitter. Falkirk police tried it by asking: 'A wall in Kinneil Drive, Bo'ness, was damaged at weekend. Black spray paint used to graffiti it. Words 'MOLLY' and 'FIONA'. Who did this?' Inevitably someone replied: 'Just a hunch. But you should maybe concentrate on looking for two women called Molly and Fiona.'

5
Relationships

Technology, politics, transport, may all be constantly changing, but the often misunderstood relationships between men and women still throw up age-old problems. Here are some.

OUR tales of romantic Glaswegians remind a reader of hearing a young chap in a city pub tell his pals: 'Yes, I love her – I'd take a bullet for her.

'Well in the leg, anyway.'

NOT everyone meets a future partner in the pub. A Newton Mearns reader was at her local gym where two other women were watching a well-muscled chap work out furiously. They were debating whether he was single, with one of them coming up with the argument: 'Of course he is. Nobody works out as hard as that when they're in a healthy relationship.'

THE chap in the Glasgow pub at the weekend was being less than chivalrous when he announced: 'The wife tells folk that twenty years after she got married, she still fits her wedding dress. What she doesn't tell them is that she was seven months pregnant at the time.'

AS Edinburgh Zoo officials, and the country's media, await news of Tian Tian's possible pregnancy, reader Gerry McDade opines: 'She lies about all day, has her accommodation and upkeep supported by the public, and her baby has two potential fathers. Why is she such big news in Scotland?'

INTERNET dating continued. A Glasgow woman was telling her pals that the latest chap she met for a meal was perhaps not too sophisticated. When she told him before ordering that she liked her meat rare, he replied: 'What? Like lions or tigers?'

A READER claims he heard a woman in Glasgow tell her pals her local jeweller's had a necklace in the sales at a great price. They asked if she bought it and she told them: 'I put a deposit down, and they said they would hold on to it until my husband did something unforgivable.'

IN the nice-try department is the young Glasgow father, whose wife was changing their new baby's nappy and who suggested that he take a turn. 'I'll do the next one,' he said from behind his newspaper. When the time came for another nappy change, his wife looked pointedly at him and he replied: 'I meant the next baby.'

WE occasionally refer to chaps who are unlucky in love. A reader tells us in his younger days when he and his friends went clubbing, one of them was given the nickname Macaulay Culkin – because he always went home alone.

AN unexpected side effect of the storm in the south of England was a group of chaps in London who had to cancel their weekly game of golf. When they later talked about what they had done instead, one of them said he had spent the day at home just chatting to his wife. He then added: 'She seems like a nice person.'

A READER says he knew he shouldn't have, but he couldn't resist it when his wife complained about his washing-up skills being inadequate while she pointed out marks on the scrubbed pots. 'The problem is that I'm a perfectionist and you're not,' she told him.

'That's why we got married,' he just had to blurt out.

DATING stories continued. A Hyndland reader says he was on a blind date which he didn't think was going well. At the end of the evening the lady asked if he wanted her phone number to get in touch again. He took out his mobile phone to put it in, but then had a sudden blank about what her name was. As he was standing there with the screen on his phone asking him to input her name, he tried the desperate trick of asking: 'How do you spell your name again?' She replied: 'M.A.R.Y.' They didn't see each other again.

A READER swears he heard a woman in a Glasgow café tell her pal that her husband had taken up riding lessons as part of a new healthy living kick. 'How's he getting on?' asked her pal.

'Judging by his size, with a crane,' said the wife.

FEARS that a Scottish education isn't what it used to be were confirmed for one reader waiting for a taxi in Glasgow's city centre last weekend, when he heard the young woman behind him in the queue tell off the young chap with her by declaring: 'The world doesn't revolve around you. You're not the moon.'

'Galileo would be so disappointed,' says our reader.

GUEST speaker Isobel Rutter, at Jewish Care's charity lunch in Giffnock, said her pals had been encouraging her to try out a dating website in order to meet a future partner. But as Isobel explained: 'I prefer to find men the old-fashioned way – through alcohol and bad judgement.'

HEARTWARMING messages don't always work in the west of Scotland. A Bishopbriggs reader tells us she copied a message she saw on an American website and texted it in a loving way to her husband. It read: 'If you are sleeping, send me your dreams. If you are laughing, send me your smile. If you are crying, send me your tears. Love you.'

He merely texted back: 'On the loo. Please advise.'

MOBILE phones continued. A woman looked at her phone and announced to her pals: 'My husband has texted me to say I was very condescending to him this morning.

'To be honest, I'm surprised he can spell it.'

BUYING underwear for your wife or girlfriend – often tricky if you are unprepared. A shop assistant in Glasgow tells us she had one gent in wishing to buy a bra for his wife. When the assistant asked what size, the customer told her: 'She wears a size four shoe. Does that help?'

'SO I said to my husband that he was putting on a bit of weight,' said the woman in the Glasgow coffee shop.

'So he said to me, "Tell me something I don't know." So I told him, "Salad is delicious."'

THE emergency powers being rushed through parliament to allow the police access to phone records was being discussed in a Glasgow pub where one toper commented: 'I'm less bothered about the police seeing my text messages than the wife.'

'WE got a baby alarm,' said the chap in the Glasgow pub the other night. 'Didn't work,' he added. 'The wife still got pregnant.'

FATHER'S DAY, and Adam Hess reminisces: 'My dad used to be at work so much during the week, I thought he was just a man who stayed at my house at weekends to give me cycling lessons.'

WE mentioned Father's Day, and Alastair Stewart passes on: 'At our Sunday Service our Minister asked the children what they had done for Father's Day. One boy immediately put up his hand and replied, "I woke him up."'

READER Stewart MacKenzie jokes: 'I noticed an advert offering tickets for Henley at £198 for food, champagne and rowing.

'For a fraction of that cost, my wife and I can go down to the local pub, have a bite to eat and a few drinks, then row all the way home.'

SOMEONE who is perhaps not long for this relationship was the chap on the London train to Glasgow who was overheard having an argument with his girlfriend on his mobile phone. It really wasn't going to get him very far when, as his voice got louder and louder, he ended the conversation with: 'And your dad thinks you're fat too,' before snapping shut his phone.

WHAT happens when mates try to be helpful? A reader on a Glasgow bus heard a young chap discuss his new girlfriend with his pal, and express his concern that she maybe went to tanning salons a bit too often. However, his pal tried to reassure him: 'The good thing is, she's so orange that snogging her would count as one of your five a day.'

A READER sitting on the train near two ladies who embarked at Whitecraigs Station realised they were discussing a woman of their acquaintance when one of them said disparagingly: 'She's more can of peas than canapés.'

A READER walking up Buchanan Street watched as a charity-type person amiably said to two young ladies walking towards him: 'Hi, can I talk to you about homelessness?' The two girls walked past him without breaking stride, and as they passed our reader he heard a snatch of their conversation, which was: 'And he kept on complaining that I was selfish. Can you believe it?'

A READER swears to us that he heard a middle-aged chap chatting up a woman in a West End bar at the weekend who told her: 'I used to be in a band called *Been There Done That.*

'You probably wore one of our t-shirts,' he added.

GETTING the bus into Glasgow, a reader heard a young woman tell her pal: 'Going out with someone just because they're good looking is so shallow. You should take other things into account – like does he have a lot of money?'

CHANGING your hair colour can throw up the occasional problem. A reader heard a young woman tell her pals in a Glasgow bar, while discussing said lady's new boyfriend: 'He told me he liked blondes. And I thought, 'Wait a minute, I'm not a blonde'. And then I remembered I was.'

NOSTALGIA alert! We asked for your dating stories, and Ian McCloy tells us of growing up in Port Glasgow where, as a nervous teenager on his first date, he sheltered down the back close of his date's tenement building. Ian says: 'Leading me to the brick-built dustbin store and out of the icy blast, my date ran her fingers over the lids of the galvanised dustbins and announced that she was going to sit on that one. "Why that one?" I asked.

"Someone has just put out the hot ashes from their fire and it will keep my backside warm" she said.'

A MILNGAVIE reader was watching his wife apply her make-up when she suddenly stopped and said: 'My face has come out in a rash.' She giggled and added: 'I look just like a teenager again.'

He now regrets replying: 'That could explain the puppy fat then.'

A REMINDER that it's Valentine's Day. Alan Barlow in Paisley was buying his wife a card and a modest bunch of flowers in his local supermarket when the woman in front of him at the checkout looked at his purchases and said in a loud voice: 'Is that all you've got?' Alan says: 'Trying to defend myself, as an older married man, I said I had done my best, but then suggested that I would take my wife out for a meal, and buy her chocolates. This seemed to amuse the queue behind me. The lady then said, "No. If that is all you've got then you can go in front of me!"'

WE hear from the STUC's Women's Conference in Dundee where Unison's splendid equality officer from Glasgow Eileen Dinning, chairing the conference, was telling the delegates about the Scottish woman on trial for murdering her husband, who was asked by the judge why she had shot him with a bow and arrow.

'I didn't want to wake the weans,' she replied.

YES, St Valentine's Day. A chap in a Glasgow pub told his pals that last year he sent his wife a bunch of flowers with the message: 'Thanks for putting up with me so long.' It caused some consternation when they arrived as the flower shop had actually put on the card 'Thanks for putting up with me. So long.'

ENJOYING the Burns Suppers? Giffnock and Newlands synagogue in East Renfrewshire held a Burns Supper for the first time in its seventy-five-year history. As one of the speakers put it: 'I said to my wife, "Did you ever in your wildest fantasies imagine I would speak at a Burns supper at the synagogue?" "Trust me," replied my wife, "you're never in my wildest fantasies."'

AND the traditional gag for St Valentine's Day is the Glaswegian who declared: 'My wife's been leaving magazines around the house left open with adverts for jewellery circled. So, I've taken the hint – it's a magazine rack for her on Valentine's Day.'

NOT everyone likes smokers, it has to be said. A Lanarkshire reader at a New Year party tells us that a young chap there kissed a girl at midnight who told him, with a certain look of disgust: 'Yuck. You smoke? It's like kissing an ashtray.'

The chap tried to preserve his dignity by telling her: 'That's some strange hobby you've got.'

'TWELFTH wedding anniversary,' said the chap in the Glasgow pub at the weekend. 'Told the wife I'd take her to the cinema. Then blew it by suggesting we see *Twelve Years A Slave*.'

THE chap in the Glasgow pub last night told his fellow topers: 'Did you see that it was so cold in Northern America that the town of Hell froze over?' 'I'm away home then,' announced one of his pals. 'You'll never guess what the wife promised me if that ever happened.'

A READER going through airport security was behind a chap who had dawdled a bit and was well behind his wife, who had already gone through. When the chap at the desk stopped him and asked for his boarding pass, the traveller said his wife had it, and bawled out: 'Margaret, come back!' The security chap turned round and said: 'Margaret. Now's your chance. Run!'

A READER was chatting to a retired minister who revealed he had recently conducted a marriage ceremony where he suddenly forgot the groom's name just as he got to the vows. He concedes that he could have worded it better when he asked the young groom: 'In what name do you come to be married today?' The groom, attempting to grasp what the reverend meant, loudly replied: 'In the name of the Father, the Son and the Holy Ghost.'

NEWS events are of course frequently discussed on the way into work. One woman on the bus into Glasgow was heard telling her pal: 'Did you see that Saatchi guy claimed that his wife Nigella Lawson was off her head on drugs?'

'You would have to be,' replied her pal, 'to wake up next to him in the morning.'

RODDY FRAME of *Aztec Camera* fame took the crowd at Glasgow's Concert Hall back to 1983, in order to play tracks from his debut album that came out thirty years ago. To help the crowd, who were all of a certain age, to get in the mood of the early eighties, Roddy told them: 'Sit back and think about the one you love; not the one you're with tonight who you're not too keen on.'

A MUIREND reader tells us a divorced friend was discussing her lack of success in the dating field when she suddenly announced: 'Do you think I'm single because I didn't pass on that chain letter I got fifteen years ago?'

JOHN PARK tells us about the chap working in a Motherwell supermarket who was stacking the shelves with washing powder. That night in the pub he was telling some girls he was chatting to that he was a member of an 'Ariel display team'.

A GLASGOW chap was being asked how he was getting on with the girl he had recently met. 'She texted me, "Your lovely", he explained to his pals, 'and I texted back, "No, YOU'RE lovely." Now I can't get rid of her, even though all I was doing was correcting her grammar.'

WE don't get many *Big Issue* stories these days as it has now become less remarkable to see people selling it. However, a reader swears to us that he heard a business chap being asked: 'Would you like a *Big Issue* pal?' He replied: 'No thanks. I'm sure my wife will already have one lined up for me when I get home.'

THE state of marriages was being discussed in a Glasgow pub the other night where one regular claimed his wife had divorced him because of arithmetic. As this just left everyone puzzled, he was asked to elucidate.

'She put two and two together,' he told them.

A PARTICK reader says she received an email from a girlfriend who had finally decided to try an Internet dating company and was now going steady with the chap she met within days of joining. Our reader thought it was rather witty that her friend wrote: 'So, you could say it was love at first site.'

A READER wonders about the young girl whom he heard in the supermarket gossiping with her girlfriend. Her pal asked her for more details. The girl then replied: 'I've already told you more than I actually know.'

THE course of true love doesn't always run smoothly. A reader on a bus heard a young man say to the young lady with him, who was concentrating on her mobile: 'You're always on your phone.'

Without looking up, she replied: 'You're always on ma nerves.'

A READER swears to us that she was at a seminar on relationships when the speaker urged the women to text their husbands to tell them they loved them.

One woman got a reply asking if she had crashed the car and another was told: 'I thought we agreed afternoon drinking was a bad idea.'

6
Politics

What a year that was. The referendum arguments seemed to be never-ending. Fortunately *Herald* readers found a few nuggets amongst the dross.

STILL GAME writer Greg Hemphill pondered the latest independence scare story from the Liberal Democrats' Scottish Secretary Alistair Carmichael, and told his fans: 'Carmichael saying today "great British institutions at risk from yes vote, including the National Lottery". No! Not the scratch cards? Please God!!'

OH yes, the referendum. Robert White passes on: 'In a Kirkcudbright pub at the weekend, a girl noticed a fella with a face she recognised tattooed on his arm. She walked up and said, 'I guess you must be a Yes supporter with a tattoo of Rabbie Burns on your arm.' The fella paused, then replied in a thick Scouse accent, "It's Bruce Lee."'

THE lighter side of the independence referendum – a 'Diary' fan in London heard a young woman tell her pal: 'If Scotland gets independence at least we'll have someone who votes for us in the Eurovision song contest.'

A SOCIETY has been formed to raise awareness of remarkable Scottish politician and writer Robert Cunninghame Graham, who not only helped found the Scottish Labour Party, but was also first president of the Scottish National Party before his death in Argentina in the 1930s. What we like about Robert is what he said more than 100 years ago with remarkable prescience. Arguing for a Scottish Parliament all those years ago he declared that what he wanted was a 'national parliament, with the pleasure of knowing that the taxes are wasted in Edinburgh instead of London.'

FORMER Socialist MSP Rosie Kane is to appear as herself when the play *I Tommy*, about Tommy Sheridan's colourful life, moves to the Glasgow Pavilion. We liked it when Rosie, who has now done a few stage appearances, described her Glasgow roots: 'We were a large family . . . like the Osmonds, but with fillings.'

COUNCILS across Scotland are sent requests for information under the Freedom of Information Act from numerous newspapers looking for stories. We hear about one council, which was asked by a newspaper: 'What is the oddest FOI question you've been asked?' The council just had to reply: 'This one.'

READER Jim McDougall tells us that one of the joys of leafleting is the signs some folk have attached to their front doors. While out in his native Largs the other day, he came across 'Visitors welcome. Family by appointment', 'All who pass through this door bring happiness; some in arriving, others in leaving' and the simple plea 'Ring bell, if no answer, pull weeds.'

GLASGOW comedian Frankie Boyle has a rant at almost everything in his book *Scotland's Jesus*. Backing independence for Scotland, Frankie argues: 'Labour's Alistair Darling described Scottish independence as a 'one-way ticket to nowhere', which is coincidentally the exact phrase I use at the Virgin counter whenever I want to travel to Newcastle. I'm not surprised the Tories in Scotland are using this phrase also, but I just thought it would be appearing as the slogan on the front of their manifesto.'

ONE of the highlights of the Glasgow Comedy Festival is the evening of New York stand-up performers flown over by United airlines. This year one of them is Dave Fulton, who on a previous trip to London tried to explain Canada to his audience. As he put it: 'Canada's only job is to protect America from ice. That's all they've got to do.

'Because we don't have a Scotland.'

BUSINESS Secretary Vince Cable visited defence firm Thales in Govan, where he tried out the latest target locator for British troops that Thales makes: 'The Sophie Lite'. We like to think that Vince, a former Glasgow councillor, picked it up and asked what it was called. 'Sophie Lite,' he was told.

'Yes, I know – but what's it called?'

WE mentioned the campaign to have a public holiday named after Margaret Thatcher. John Harding tells us she would not be the first politician to be so honoured. 'Home Secretary Theresa May,' he tells us, 'already has a bank holiday named after her.'

MUCH merriment over the Ukip councillor claiming that recent floods were caused by the Government legalising same-sex marriages. Almost immediately a spoof Ukip Weather Twitter account was set up giving weather warnings such as: 'Council gritters are on high alert after a man in Peterborough went into a pub and ordered a glass of white wine.'

OUTRAGEOUS independence arguments, continued. An Edinburgh reader reminds us of the Fringe performer, Lee Nelson, who publicised his show about the Union, by releasing a huge balloon on which was printed: 'Scottish Independence? You'll regret it when you're sober.'

SCOTTISH Secretary Alistair Carmichael was drawing the raffle at the Glasgow Islay Gaelic Choir's concert in Milngavie at the weekend when he announced a prize of a £50 Marks and Spencer voucher, which got a large murmur of approval from the audience. 'You can tell it's Milngavie,' Alistair told them. 'When it was Partick, the voucher was for Lidl.'

RETIRED Maryhill Labour MP Maria Fyfe launched her auto-biography, *A Problem Like Maria*, in which she tells of a Glasgow MP who wanted to send a letter to the blind Government Minister David Blunkett, and went to the trouble of having it put into Braille. Well done, we say. However, when he got the Braille copy back, he then faxed it.

MARIA writes about many of the important subjects debated in Parliament, but somehow our eyes are drawn to the tale of her being asked how she found the time to do all her own washing and ironing of her clothes at her London flat while at Westminster. Maria writes: 'Well, it's not difficult. You can compose questions or a speech in your head while doing the washing up or the ironing. But one other Glasgow member, who shall remain nameless, said he had a better idea, "You know these huge, super-sized stamped envelopes we get? I put my socks, pants and shirts in them and send them up to my wife, and they're ready for me when I go home at the weekend."'

QUEEN'S Speech in Parliament. Our political contact calls to say: 'The thing about the public's perception of the Tories these days is that when the Queen's Speech includes a Modern Slavery Bill you have to stop to think whether the Government is opposing it or bringing it in.'

A POSTSCRIPT to Glasgow politician Maria Fyfe's autobiography *A Problem Like Maria*. In it she recalls Tory grandee Nicholas Soames, grandson of Winston Churchill, standing for election in Clydebank. His cause wasn't helped by the SNP publishing a photo of him winning a polo match, holding aloft the trophy brimming with Champagne, his horse on one side, a blonde beauty on the other.

Knocking doors in Clydebank, Nicholas was finding little support until in one multi-storey, a chap said he would vote Conservative. Astonished, Nicholas asked him why, and he replied: 'Any man who likes horses, booze and women can't be all that bad.'

SO anti-immigration Ukip did well in the European election. A reader remarked in his local that the election turnout in Romania was a respectable 32.2% and added: 'That's very high considering they're all supposed to be in the UK, if you listen to Ukip.'

'Postal votes,' replied someone further up the bar.

MANY folk are still in shock after right-wing Ukip took a Euro seat in Scotland. As one young Glasgow chap was heard explaining it to a pal yesterday: 'See Ukip, it's like *Coldplay* the band. Everyone says in public they hate them, but somebody must be buying their rubbish records. It's tragic.'

EUROPEAN elections. A supporter of the right-wing Ukip party asked folk to put on Twitter why they were voting for the party. Naturally, it was too good a chance to miss for those not enamoured by the allegedly racist party. Our favourite replies include: I'm voting Ukip because: 'I once ate some French cheese that gave me a tummy ache and because I'm incompetent enough to fear that my job actually might be taken by an unqualified Romanian who doesn't speak English.'

But the most inspired was Sanjeev Kohli who wrote: 'Because I'm hoping they'll repatriate my dad to India via Dubai, and I need a new digital camera.'

WE asked for your lighter moments in the independence debate, and a reader tells us: 'My anti-Tory mate told me that David Cameron begging Scots to stay in the UK is a bit like when someone posh says at a boring party: "Stay, we're going to play charades later."'

INDEPENDENCE humour continued. Stand-up Jo Caulfield, appearing at The Stand as part of the Glasgow Comedy Festival, was asked if she feels she has to mention the independence debate in her act. Jo said: 'I don't feel that I 'have' to talk about the independence referendum – it's more a case that I want to. Having watched the Nicola Sturgeon/Johann Lamont debate I'll probably be approaching it from the 'Scotland needs better dentists' angle.'

MANY and varied are the arguments for and against independence. John Watters in Greenock tells us: 'A teacher friend had a mock referendum with his class of sixteen- and seventeen-year-olds to gauge the thoughts of our young voters. After pretty much a 50/50 split, he asked two of the 'No' voters, two girls seated together, to explain their views. They said they 'couldn't live in a different country to One Direction – the boy band – and therefore would vote No'.

REMEMBER to vote in the European elections? Edinburgh comedian Ben Verth tells us: 'It's a bit sad really. I only voted because I hoped there would be some mad Ukip nutter at the polling station, so that I'd get some material for my Edinburgh Fringe show.'

INDEPENDENCE oddities continued. Peter Meager in Cupar tells us: 'I was on the Plymouth to Roscoff ferry and handed the girl on the till at the cafeteria a £20 Scottish note. She took it without hesitation, then blurted out, "Goodness, I didn't know that independence had gone through and you had your own currency now".'

A COLLEAGUE wanders over to tell us: 'What's so good about England? Well, for a start the flag is a big plus.'

WE continue our search for some humour in the independence debate. Writer and performer Sanjeev Kohli mused to his Twitter followers: 'There's a spare unit between our local fishmongers and ironmongers. Perhaps Better Together would like to open a scaremongers there?'

ALISON CAMPBELL is concerned about the possible go-ahead of the controversial gas extraction method of fracking, which opponents claim can cause earthquakes, on the shores of the River

Forth. Alison asks: 'Will people end up saying, "Did the Airth move for you?"'

DAFT independence arguments, continued. We mentioned the shopping bag with the three boxes to tick, 'Aye', 'Naw', and 'Whit's a Referendum?' On a similar vein, a Glasgow reader saw a t-shirt with a saltire on it and 'Referendum 2014' below it. There were also three boxes that could be ticked – 'Yes', 'No', and 'Either Way We're screwed'.

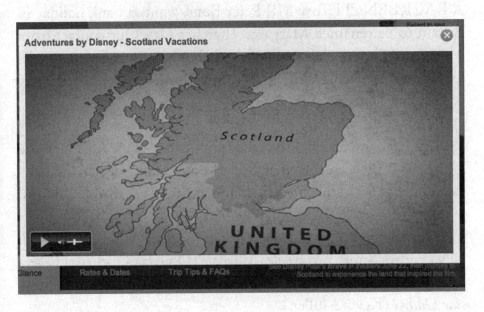

AND I'm voting in a most peculiar way . . . singer David Bowie's plea at the music awards – 'Scotland, stay with us' – has brought forward suggestions from readers on what songs he could have on his next album to appeal to Scottish fans: *Ziggy Played Stranraer. The Man Who Fell to Perth. Let's Banff. Spar Man. Jim Jimmy. All the Young Teams. Is there life on deep-fried Mars?*

AS you may know, there are many spoof Twitter accounts out there. So we suspect that the Iain Duncan Smith MP who Tweeted this was not the real Tory Cabinet minister. It said: 'Cobra Meeting to discuss floods. Have suggested people move to their second homes while main ones dry out.'

TALKING of the bad weather, an Ayrshire reader heard a theory: 'We were discussing the inclement weather in the south when a friend piped up, 'Aye, it's like the seven plagues in biblical Egypt – God's way of telling the English, "Let my people go."'

A BACKBENCH Tory MP, Peter Bone, wants a bank holiday in Britain to be renamed Margaret Thatcher Day. Our contact from what remains of the left wing of the Labour Party in Scotland tells us: 'There's no need. With current Government policies, every day is Thatcher Day these days.'

POLITICS, and an English reader phones to tell us: 'Although the Ukip party now accepts that bongo bongo land doesn't actually exist, I bet you it's still above Scotland in the FIFA world rankings.'

WE complete our David Bowie album for Scots with: *Sufferin-Eck City* (Forbes Smith) *Maybole, Maybole* (Douglas Gilchrist).*Ciders from Bars* (Frances Woodward) *Hunky Doric* (Mike Ritchie) *Speyside Oddity* (Kevin Mullen).

7

Holidays

Sometimes it's only the thought of having a holiday that keeps folk going until the summer. Here are the stories they came back with.

A READER back from holiday in Spain realised that the couple lying next to them at the hotel pool were from Glasgow when the chap, who was admittedly very hirsute on his back, asked his wife to rub some sun-tan oil on him. After a few seconds of rubbing, she exclaimed loudly in an unmistakable west coast accent: 'Ma goad, Robert. It's like rubbing custard on a shag-pile carpet.'

SOME folk are trying to lose weight before they go on holiday. A reader having a coffee in Paisley heard two women at the next table discuss a mutual friend, with one complaining: 'She said she lost six pounds last week. Six pounds! The only time I lost six pounds in one week was when I gave birth.'

AS tourists begin to make their way to Scotland for the summer, we doff our hat to the tour guides.

We recall, for example, the Glasgow tour guide pointing out the site of the Battle of Langside, where Mary, Queen of Scots suffered a bloody defeat. 'Why was it fought there?' asked a visitor. 'Handy for the Victoria Infirmary,' replied the guide.

BILL HALL, in Largs, was on a tour of the inspiring neo-gothic Mount Stuart House on Bute when the tour guide asked at the end: 'Are there any questions?' There was a silence, which was then broken by a Scottish woman at the back who spoke up: 'Where did you get your earrings?'

DAVID CAMPBELL tells us: 'On the coach journey from the ferry point at Craignure to Tobermory, the driver pointed out local landmarks including the garden of a roadside cottage which had, allegedly, the best lawn on Mull.

'He explained that the owner regularly sprayed his lawn with the finest malt whisky.

'Mind you,' he said. 'He drinks it first.'

ELMA STEVENSON tells us she was at the Corrie Golf Club tearoom on Arran when the waitress told her that she was surprised by a customer who came in with her own food and merely asked for a cup of hot water for her tea bag. Trying to think of a reason for such parsimony Elma asked the waitress: 'Was she coeliac?' 'No,' replied the lady in the tearoom. 'She came from Edinburgh.'

TOUR guides continued. John Brunton in Llandudno says: 'On a tour of Belfast, the guide pointed to a restaurant explaining that it was owned by celebrity chef Paul Rankin, whom he described to those not familiar with the name as, "Famous chef, long hair, and a big knife."

'He then said that should you be out on the town that evening and meet someone with long hair and a big knife, not to assume that it was Paul Rankin.'

A READER on holiday in Argyll popped into a local shop to buy a *Herald* and found himself stuck behind a local woman who was blethering nineteen-to-the-dozen with the assistant.

Our reader waited as patiently as he could, but just as he was about to interrupt, the woman's husband silently pulled a sweet out of his pocket and handed it to her. At that she stopped talking and popped it in her mouth, allowing our reader to be served. As the man with the garrulous lady turned to leave he muttered: 'You're welcome' to our *Herald* purchaser.

TOUR guides continued. Kenneth Morin in Newton Mearns says: 'On a tour in China with other Brits and North Americans, our tour guide told us that the seats we had on the coach were the ones we would have for the duration of the tour. She explained that this was so that she could recognise and get to know us as "we all looked the same to her."'

SCHOOL holidays of course, so it's unusual it hasn't started raining. A Dundee reader tells us: 'Overheard my neighbour saying to her son: "You've been off school for only two days and I'm already done with this."'

A READER fed up with folk going on about their holidays tells us: 'Pretend you're on holiday in France by going to a baker's twice a day like you've never seen a baker's before.'

WE mentioned tour guides, and Jock Laidlaw from Lockerbie recalls: 'I did an open-topped bus tour of Dublin when the guide announced at one point, "The Taoiseach is a very fine man called Brian Cowen, currently doing the job of two men." He then added, "Laurel and Hardy."'

TOUR guides continued. Moyna Gardner in Glasgow tells us: 'On a bus tour of Ireland, the driver kept talking about the misdeeds of the 'Anglo-Normans'. It puzzled me until at last I realised this was his way of describing the English without offending all the English people on the bus.'

OUR tour guide stories remind Sonia Petersen, in Glasgow, of travelling on the *Jacobite* steam train to Mallaig with her sister Eva when the guide announced: 'Ladies and gentleman, please get your cameras ready for the famous Glenfinnan viaduct.' As everyone rushed to the windows, Eva scanned the sky and shouted: 'I can't see them!' 'What?' asked her confused sister. 'The flying ducks!' replied Eva, and then wondered why the whole carriage was laughing.

BILL ALLAN from Stonehaven was walking past the town's Tolbooth Museum when he was stopped by an American tourist who asked him what the large object was outside the museum's door.

Says Bill: 'I replied that it was a mangle, and when she asked me what it was for, I said that in the past it was used to take the water out of clothes after they were washed. She said, "Ok, ya mean it's a spin cycle?"'

JOHN PARK in Motherwell has returned from an Easter holiday on Tenerife where the Scottish comic doing a turn at the hotel was aware that there were children in the audience despite it being a late show. John says: 'The first thing he said was, "Now children, if any of you inadvertently repeat any of my sweary, bad words in class, just tell the teacher it's Spanish – a primary school teacher won't know the difference."'

WE like how Scots think on their feet. Paul Drury tells us he was on the P&O cruise-ship *Ventura* at Corsica, when a passenger who explained she was 'Annette fae Macduff' was chosen by the ship's entertainer as the best dancing granny in a fun contest on deck. When she was then asked if she was delighted with her prize of a special cruise cocktail she quickly replied: 'Aye – but there's four of us.'

OUR tour guide stories remind Bob Craig in Campbeltown of the boss of City Sightseeing bus tours in Glasgow once explaining that he sat on one of his open-topped buses and listened to the tour guide giving her spiel.

He wondered if visitors preferred her to the buses using a recorded commentary, so he asked the Glasgow couple sitting opposite if they had deliberately chosen a bus with a live guide.

Bob says: 'The husband was slightly puzzled by the question and replied, "Well, she wouldn't be much good if she wuz deid."'

AND former Glasgow tour guide Gordon Hogg, now in Alicante, tells us: 'There was the old perennial, regularly used by a colleague,

'Up there is Glasgow Necropolis, where the inventor of the cross-word puzzle is buried.

'You'll have no trouble finding his grave – it's four rows across, and six down.'

NOT everyone had great weather this summer. As reader Stuart Roberts in Switzerland opines: 'Looking back over summer, I'm left wondering why is it that the only thing that got tanned was my Visa card.'

A JORDANHILL reader tells us: 'When we were young, we went to North Berwick every year. One year my sister and I said we would like to go somewhere else but my father said we had nothing to complain about as the holiday destination was chosen democratically.

'I told him I didn't remember ever taking a vote and he told me, "Of course not. Children don't get to vote."'

GORDON PHILLIPS in Ayr tells us about a recent Caribbean cruise where an American passenger buttonholed the captain to tell him she was quite alarmed to see some water coming down the stairs. The skipper cheerfully told her it was nothing to worry about – but if she ever saw water going up the stairs she should contact him immediately.

WORD from the countryside is that the midges are bad this year. Reader Willie McNish says he was in a shop in Whiting Bay when a local contractor, working in a glen where the little blighters are particularly vicious, was trying to describe conditions. 'I saw one with a sheep in its mouth,' he told fellow shoppers with a straight face.

A GLASGOW reader on a climbing trip to Africa was telling friends he was bitten by a snake and went to the local hospital for a check-up as a precaution. 'Are you allergic to anything?' the doctor asked and the chap said he couldn't stand needles. At that, the doctor brought out one of the largest syringes the climber had ever seen, and he fainted on the spot.

When he came to and asked the doctor what he was playing at, the medic replied: 'I thought you said noodles.'

DONALD PARK in Motherwell was on holiday in Tenerife where he got into conversation with a Glaswegian staying in a nearby hotel. Spotting that the Glasgow chap was wearing an 'all-inclusive' wristband for the hotel, Donald asked him why he was out paying for his drink in the bar.

'I'm not really all-inclusive,' revealed the Glaswegian. 'I just bought this band for 50 cents and wrote a room number on it with a felt tip pen. It saves me 35 Euros a day.'

8

Senior Citizens

We all grow old, obviously. Fortunately our sense of humour does not diminish with age, as our readers show.

A READER tells us about taking an elderly relative to Crosshouse Hospital, Kilmarnock, where the doctor taking notes asked her for her next-of-kin's telephone number. 'That will be my daughter,' she replied.

'And the phone number?' asked the doctor.

'Button one,' she told him.

A READER at a charity dinner tells us a guest speaker was a surgeon from Glasgow who said he once had to operate on his own father. Before he was anaesthetised his dad told him: 'Don't be nervous – just remember if something happens to me, your mother is going to come and live with you.'

BUS passes for pensioners are greatly appreciated in Scotland, but they can be a bit tricky at first. Robin Gilmour in Milngavie explains: 'A friend of mine was telling me about the first time he used his bus pass. Having entered the charabanc, he got himself in a right old muddle as to where he put his card, much to the frustration of the driver, not to mention folk behind him as it was raining.

'When at last he made his way towards his seat, a young lad, as my friend was passing, said, "Your chauffeur's day aff, big man?"'

GROWING old continued. A reader in Jordanhill tells us: 'It really is hard to convey to young people the excitement we all genuinely felt at school when the teacher wheeled in an overhead projector to the classroom.'

A READER getting the bus into Glasgow was much taken with a couple of pensioners behind him discussing a mutual friend. 'She saw a pair of shoes she fancied in the charity shop, but said they were too dear.'

'Too dear in a charity shop?' replied her pal. 'What's she going to do, then? Rummage through bins?'

A GP swears to us that a patient came in complaining about a terrible pain in his big toe.

'Gout,' the doctor told him.

'But I've only just got here,' the patient replied.

WE can become a tad forgetful as we get older. A Milngavie pensioner parked his car in the car park behind the King's Theatre in Glasgow, and had to jump out to check he was within the parking bay. Anyway, after attending a play at the theatre for three hours he couldn't find his car keys – he even got the assistant to check the row with her torch.

He then headed back to his car thinking he may have dropped the keys, and there they were in the ignition – with the engine still running.

A JORDANHILL reader gardening at the weekend heard his wife who was watering the flowers slap herself then shout over: 'Why can't midgies suck out fat instead of blood?'

A READER was in a health food store at the Silverburn shopping centre, when an elderly lady following her daughter around looked at all the bottles on the shelves and announced: 'When I was young vitamins only went up to C.'

PEOPLE get quite excited when they turn sixty and qualify for their free bus pass. As one west-ender in Glasgow told his pals: 'I now qualify for my bus pass. Only drawback is the drivers who shout at me as if I'm deaf and senile.

'Luckily I am.'

SO many people want to be comedians, it seems. A south-side reader says he was in his doctor's waiting room, when an elderly gent came in, flicked through a magazine on the table, and announced: 'Oh no! Winston Churchill's dead!'

WE mentioned growing concerns about elderly drivers, and a Dunblane reader tells us about his father-in-law who got lost between Ayr and Dunblane, and ended up in Bishopbriggs, eventually arriving home hours late. When his family questioned him on how he ended up in Bishopbriggs, he blamed the taxi he was following. 'But why did you follow the taxi?' asked his family.

'Because I reckoned he would know where he was going,' came the indignant reply.

'I'M getting old,' announced a chap in a Glasgow pub the other day. 'The guys in the office were discussing which of the female staff would you like to get stuck in a lift with. I told them, "The one who knows how to fix lifts."'

A NEW savings bond for the over-sixty-fives announced in the Budget has been dubbed the 'pensioner bond'. A Motherwell reader says his pensions adviser revealed it is now known in the industry as a 'Sean Connery'.

ROBIN GILMOUR in Milngavie tells us that a friend was telling his wife that he was thinking of joining the local ramblers' club. 'Is that walking or talking?' she rather unkindly inquired.

WORRIES about elderly drivers continued. A Coatbridge reader tells us he discussed with his mother-in-law the fact that her husband had failed to stop at red lights. Trying to defend hubby, she replied: 'Yes, but not every one!'

'Eventually,' says our reader, who reveals his plot to force his dangerous father-in-law off the road, 'we disconnected the coil in the car, and sold it when it wouldn't start.'

COLIN MUNRO was in Larkhall when the elderly lady beside him was shouting across the busy main street to a pal who had difficulty making out what she was saying. Eventually the pal crossed over the road and declared: 'Ken Wilma, am gettin' that deef ah canny even lip read.' Colin is still trying to work that one out.

MORE on forgetfulness with Bill Garven telling us he was in a car park beside his Honda Civic when he pressed the remote control on his key, and a car at the other end of the car park beeped its horn and flashed its lights in response.

Bill says: 'Striding purposefully towards the other car, already making up my letter of complaint to Honda and simply to take a note of the car registration number, imagine my surprise to discover it had the same registration plate as my own.'

A POLL released shows that over one-third of Scots are concerned about the driving skills of an elderly relative. It reminds us of the gag about the pensioner stopped for driving far too slowly on the M8. When the police asked why she was crawling along she said she thought the sign M8 meant she had to go at eight miles an hour.

The old fella beside her looked a bit faint, and when the cops asked if he was okay, he told them they had just come off the M90.

FORGETFUL continued. Robert Gardner says: 'My aunt wanted to go to the old Lewis's in Glasgow, and my uncle being a pipe smoker said he would stand outside and wait for her coming out. Clasping lots of parcels after a successful day, she got the train home, and as she put the key in the door, realised that she had left her other half in

Glasgow. She phoned the shop in a panic, and he was still patiently waiting at the door. She never was allowed to forget that.'

A GLASGOW doctor tells us he was in awe of his receptionist when she gave a patient phoning in for an appointment to see the doctor a time slot in three days' time. When the agitated patient replied: 'Three days! Ah could be dead by then!' She calmly replied: 'In that case would someone be able to phone and cancel the appointment?'

WISE words from a pensioner who was telling his pals: 'Night-time when you're elderly and living alone can be terrifying. Windows rattle, stairs creak, and most worrying of all, the boiler starts up.'

A SOUTH-SIDE reader heard a pensioner at the bus stop the other day tell her pal that she was going to spend a day next week going round the city by bus to hand-deliver her Christmas cards.

With astute logic she explained: 'With stamps now 50p, and the bus for free, it will save me a fortune.'

WE asked about being forgetful, and Glen Elliot from Elgin recalls parking in an Inverness multi-storey car park and carefully noting they were beside a number five on the wall, next to a large pillar. Glen says: 'On returning we located number five and the large pillar, but no car. I summoned the car park attendant who looked at our parking ticket and said, "First of all, you are on the wrong level. Number five is the speed limit on all floors and the large pillar is the same on all levels." I found my car and promised to go by train next time.'

AFTER *The Herald* news story about 'white coat syndrome' whereby people give high blood-pressure readings because of being nervous in front of a doctor, Jim Slavin in Blackness muses: 'As an occasional visitor to Golden Jubilee and Forth Valley Royal Hospitals, the only people I have seen wearing white coats have been the guys from Magee's Bakery delivering the rolls.'

A SENIOR citizen on Glasgow's south-side was celebrating his eighty-fifth birthday the other day with family and friends gathered round when a cake was brought in with candles for him to blow out. As he completed the Herculean task the cry went up for him to 'make a wish!' The short silence that followed was broken by the old chap's wife declaring: 'Nope. Still here.'

KILMAURS reader John Bannerman was unhappy when he called in at his doctor's surgery and was told he would have to see a vet. When he went into the room indicated a new doctor at the practice introduced herself as Yvette. He now wonders whether he should add hearing difficulties to the reasons for his visit.

OUR mention of cardiac rehabilitation classes reminds Tom Law of attending one where an ageing chap was being told by the nurse how many weeks it would be before he could drive a car, and how many weeks it would be before he could have sex.

'That's some operation,' he told her. 'I've never had a driving licence – and as for sex . . . well the last time was about fifteen years ago.'

A PRESTWICK reader passes on: 'While visiting my aunt in a Glasgow hospital, a very neat, young, stylish and well-spoken dietician entered the ward.

'She approached a very thin, frail wee old lady and in her poshest Bearsden accent said, "And why do we think you may be losing weight?" At this, the wee old lady replied simply, "Ahm no eatin hen."'

OUR story of the priest in the hospital mistaking the abbreviation Cath (for catheter) beside patients' names, as signifying they were Catholic, reminds John Newlands: 'As a nurse in the Beatson I was approached by an irate nun complaining about our new patient notice board. I explained that 'P' after each name meant porridge, 'C' cornflakes and the less than receptive patient she had approached was a devotee of Rice Crispies.'

A CHAP who moved to the north of Scotland recently picked up an elderly relative who came to visit, and as they drove along to their house off a single-track road, he courteously waved at every driver who pulled in to let him pass. When they arrived at the house his relative told his wife approvingly: 'You've only been here a short time but already Alan seems to know everyone up here.'

JIMMY MANSON tells us: 'I parked my car at Ayr Hospital and an official said to me: "You can't park there, it's for badge holders only." I replied: "Well I'm here to see about my bad shoulder."'

OUR story about dental appointments provokes a reader in Elgin: 'Women's logic – my wife has just returned from the dentist. I asked her how her new dentures were doing.

'She replied, "Oh fine, I'm leaving them out until I get used to them."'

9

School

Nor should we forget that the youngest amongst us can be just as funny as their elders.

A FORMER St Aloysius pupil in Glasgow tells us: 'Back in the late 1950s we had swimming lessons one morning each week, and had to sprint down through Cowcaddens to the local public pool, and woe betide any stragglers. The PE teacher was a wee hard man and took no prisoners.

'One luckless lad was seen to be getting changed rather too slowly and he was picked up and hurled half-dressed into the pool. As he sailed through the air he yelled the immortal line, "Ah'm no' at your school."'

OUT of the mouths of babes ... Alex Findlay was at the Laigh Kirk in Kilmarnock when the minister asked one of the little ones from the Sunday School: 'How old are you?' 'Four,' the little one replied. 'When will you be five?' the minister continued.

'When I'm finished with being four,' said the youngster with impeccable logic.

HALF of primary pupils cannot swim, leading to calls for more lessons at school. It reminds us of the Edinburgh PE teacher who took a class to the baths, and sent one girl, whose costume was covered in proficiency badges, to the deep end.

She immediately got into difficulties, and he had to dive in to save her. Once out the pool he asked about her awards and she told him: 'Oh, them. The cossie's my sister's.'

GREAT apologies of our time. 'In an article in the *Cumbernauld News* and *Kilsyth Chronicle* issue of 2 July 2014, we stated that Caitlin Henderson and her friend Calum Robinson were 'the envy of their classmates' when they arrived for their school prom at Condorrat Primary School.

'However, Mrs Alison Masterson contacted us to say that her daughter was not 'envious'. We are happy to set the record straight and apologise for any embarrassment it may have caused.'

A CLARKSTON reader tells us she caught her four-year-old daughter lifting some grapes from her younger sister's plate. 'Are you stealing your sister's grapes?' demanded mum.

'No,' she replied. 'I'm teaching her to share.'

PALM Sunday, commemorating when Jesus rode into Jerusalem. Richard Fowler in Kirkwall, Orkney, tells us: 'The lady giving the children's address at our church service asked, "Today has a special name. Do you know what it is?"

'As she was met with silence and heads being shaken, she said, "I'll give you a clue. Two words. First word—" and raised her hand, palm faced towards the children. At that point one child yelled excitedly, "High five!"'

AFTER *The Herald* news story about the private school in Rutherglen having financial difficulties, reader Mark Boyle opines: 'I'm not surprised. No matter what the Coalition or Alex Salmond says, no matter what the banks say about green shoots of recovery, when you see a kid in a Hutchie Grammar blazer doing a paper round, you know the economy just isn't there.'

JOHN MACDONALD says a pupil in his daughter-in-law's class was pulled up for not doing his homework.

The boy claimed he had left his homework on a chair in the sitting room and went out. When he came back his granny was sitting in the chair fast asleep – and he didn't have the heart to wake her.

EXCUSES, more of. 'Your stories about excuses at school reminded me of the young teacher whose first teaching post was in Lockerbie Academy,' Bob Byiers writes.

'Shortly after starting, he was nonplussed one morning when a pupil in his register class offered as an excuse for his late arrival that the "feckin bus was late."

'He was relieved to learn later that this was the local jargon for the bus that came from Ecclefechan.'

STRANGE excuses, continued. When Phil Cairney was a teacher in Pollok he had a registration class first thing in the morning. One girl arrived late and Phil wanted to know why. She told him: 'I was dreaming about Celtic.'

'Why would that make you late?' asked a baffled Phil.

'The game went into extra time, sir,' came the reply.

HOW things have changed. Barrie Crawford tells us a friend in her fifties bumped into her old physics teacher, and as she told Barrie: 'There were two girls in the class and he called us both Daphne. He couldn't be bothered learning our names, because he thought girls shouldn't be doing physics.'

JUNE already, and it will soon be the school summer holidays. A reader tells us he was in a west-end newsagent's this time last year when a primary teacher he knew rushed in and bought a whole box of chocolate bars.

She explained she was giving them to her pupils on the last day of term, and as she was a bit rushed he asked her why she hadn't bought them in advance.

'I did,' she replied. 'then ate my way through them every night when I came home from school.'

SCOTTISH pupils have just done their maths exam at Higher and something called National Fives. One Bearsden parent tells us when he asked his son how he got on, he thought about it for a moment before replying: 'I think what's important is that we have our health.'

OUR story about the school history exam reminds Russell Vallance in Helensburgh: 'My friend's daughter was recently teaching on the effects of World War One. She asked the class: "What was something specific Germany was made to do at the end of the war?" One girl answered: "They had to hand back Alice and Lorraine." Through splutters, the teacher asked who she thought Alice and Lorraine were. "I guess two French girls kidnapped by the Germans before the war, Miss."'

THE *Herald* news story that academics want to revive interest in studying Latin in Scottish primary schools reminds a Glasgow teacher of telling her class that the word 'ante' was the Latin for before, and could the pupils give any examples of it being used in a word. A hand popped up and a child eagerly told her 'Antifreeze!' 'Not quite,' replied the teacher, but the young one persisted: 'Yes, you put it in your car before it freezes.'

INCIDENTALLY, a history teacher tells us he was tempted to give a mark to the pupil in the exam who, when asked 'What ended in 1918?' wrote '1917'.

A BISHOPBRIGGS grandfather was taken aback when his granddaughter, watching the popular animated film *Frozen* on the telly, suddenly announced 'I want a figure of Anna or else!' He was trying to remonstrate with her about making such demands when his daughter gently explained to him that the main characters in the film were Anna and Elsa.

WISE words heard by a reader in a Clarkston coffee shop where a woman was telling her pal that she was worried that her young son seemed a bit on the short side for his age. 'Buy him an expensive new blazer,' her pal recommended, presumably from experience, 'and watch him shoot up.'

THE student library at St Andrews University has suggestion boxes so that those studying can raise questions about opening hours, heating and so on. Just recently someone put in the box: 'There aren't enough cute boys here!' Which is why on the University's website, the assistant director of libraries has patiently explained: 'Lack of provision of cute boys – I'm afraid, I don't think we're going to be able to introduce a policy of entrance to the Library being dependent on users' relative levels of cuteness. It's an interesting prospect but I fear would be impractical to enforce, not least because what one person finds cute may not be the same for someone else. The subjective nature of human attraction I suppose.'

FIRST day yesterday of the new National Five exams in Scotland's secondary schools. An exam website lists answers given by either inspired or desperate pupils to questions given in previous tests, which included: Name six animals that live specifically in the Arctic – Two polar bears, four seals.

Explain the phrase 'free press' – When your mum irons trousers for you.

To change centimetres to metres you must? – Take out centi.

THE BBC news covered the opening of a new exhibition on the Vikings dispelling the popularly held view that they wore horned helmets. Never happened apparently. It reminds Barrie Crawford: 'I was talking to a history teacher at St Pat's in Coatbridge. One day he had to cover for an absent colleague and the topic was the Vikings. He told the class that Vikings, contrary to popular belief, did not have horns on their helmets. One bright lad asked him, "Please, sir, are you sure you're a proper history teacher?"'

OUTRAGEOUS spelling errors continued. Joe Marshall in Edinburgh recalls marking prelim exams where there was a question on limestone caverns. One pupil put forward the interesting theory that 'starling tights' hung from the roof of such caverns.

TRANSLATIONS continued. Retired modern languages teacher Garry Larkin tells us that one year in the Higher French paper the phrase 'les minces peupliers frissonnaient dans la nuit' which should have been translated as 'the thin poplars rustled in the night' came back from some pupils as 'the people were frying mince in the night.' Adds Garry: 'After that, dictionaries were allowed.'

POSTSCRIPT to our spelling howlers, as Tom Hamilton tells us: 'I remember from my distant days in academe at Strathclyde

Uni, Professor Tom Devine, then just a plain old Dr, said that one undergraduate, when writing an essay on the French Revolution, referred to the infamous sovereign lady as 'Mary-Anne Twanette'.

FRENCH translations continued. Cora Snyder tells us: 'My mother was amused at a pupil's translation of '*un grand châtaignier agité par le vent*' (*châtaignier* – chestnut tree) as 'a large tom-cat troubled with wind'. She said she wished she could give an extra mark for the sheer entertainment value.'

MATTHEW SPICER tells us: 'My daughter's flatmate at university missed a philosophy lecture and borrowed the notes of a colleague who was thought to be thorough in these matters. They contained a comprehensive account of the work of the hitherto neglected female Greek philosopher, Iris Dottle.'

OUTRAGEOUS spelling mistakes, and Tom Bradshaw in Bellshill recalls: 'Many years ago I came across a pupil who entered a piece of graffiti on the cover of his history jotter: '1690 – Remember the Boing'.'

SCHOOL spelling howlers continued. Says Roy Henderson in Blairgowrie: 'During a lesson on descriptive writing, one of my younger pupils had me initially puzzling over an item of furniture in her room called the Chester Draws. Ever since then, the similar piece of furniture in our own bedroom has been called Chester.'

WE asked about school punishments after the belt was banned, and Angela Simms recalls: 'I was a teacher then in Possilpark. As the phasing out of corporal punishment was introduced I told a fourth-year boy, who had been carrying on, that he had the choice of either writing 100 lines or writing a story about what he could do to behave better in class. He thought about these choices for a minute then said, "Aw, miss, gonnae just gie us the belt? If ah go hame wi' lines, ma da will only hit me onyway fur getting them'".

WILD misspellings continued. Bob Byiers recalls when pupils wrote essays about their summer holidays. Says Bob: 'One boy wrote that he had been to Rossie, and was severely reprimanded for not being able to spell Rothesay properly. Eventually he managed to persuade the teacher that he had in fact spent his summer at Rossie which was what we called in those days an approved school, near Montrose.'

SCHOOL spelling errors, and Nita Marr in Longniddry, East Lothian, recalls her daughter going to a fancy-dress party, in an outfit made out of dozens of ties, as 'Miss Tieland'. However, when she wrote about it at school the following week, the teacher corrected it to 'Miss Thailand'.

'So, your teacher didn't see the punny side of it,' Nita told her daughter.

KEVIN WYBER, who is producing the show *The Mungo Boys*, following the lives of former pupils of Glasgow's St Mungo's Academy, tells us the old Townhead school had a separate staircase for the teachers, nicknamed the Scala Sancta, and woe betide any pupil who tried to use it.

Legend has it, says Kevin, that the then heidie, nicknamed Farmer Kelly, mistook a fresh-faced new teacher on his first day of school as a pupil and belted him for using the stairs.

WE hear about a first-year geography class where the teacher was talking about the relative size of cities, towns and villages when she asked: 'Does anybody know the name of a settlement that's even smaller than that? Just a row of houses?' One young girl, who had perhaps just come from her English class, excitedly threw her hand up triumphantly and declared: 'A Macbeth!'

WE asked for school punishments that didn't involve the belt, and Andrea Christie in West Dunbartonshire says: 'Jordanhill teacher training did not include lessons on effective use of the belt and we were left to devise our own methods. I was a home economics teacher who could never master the technique and quickly devised a punishment for pupils bigger than me – they were instructed to chop onions.'

A PRIMARY teacher has promised to work on spelling with her class after a young one wrote that her family had visited a house owned by Jookabukloo. Her original thoughts were, perhaps a rap star, until she finally worked out it was Scotland's biggest landowner, the Duke of Buccleuch.

The wild spellings of pupils remind Jimmy Lynch: 'My old professor told us a paper by one of his students constantly referred to the Aegean Sea which he rendered as the 'Ag and C'. So much for higher education.'

OUR mention of school belts reminds Colin Castle: 'When I was at Kingsridge Secondary School in Drumchapel the belt of a fellow teacher vanished and he suspected one pupil from his register class. He told them he would leave the room and return in five minutes and if the belt was on his desk no more would be said about it.

'After the allotted time, he returned and the belt was indeed on his desk – but in a pile of half-inch square chunks. Presumably the culprit had acquired a Stanley knife from the technical department and performed surgery before returning it.'

SWIMMING baths continued. Matt Vallance tells us of a contemporary who trained as a PE teacher at Jordanhill in Glasgow in the 1960s when he was sent to one of the city's more challenging schools. Taking the boys to the local baths he told one of those assembled at the side of the pool to take his socks off before getting in.

He then realised that hygiene may be a future topic of discussion as the lad replied: 'Please sur, ah hiv taken aff ma socks'.

MORE on Glasgow's St Mungo's Academy and infamous belter Farmer Kelly. Says Paul Cortopassi in Bonnybridge: 'He was not the most popular teacher as he belted you at the slightest provocation. He was also a dedicated follower of Queen's Park FC – or the 'jolly old Queens' as he called them. One day he heard a strange noise from his desk and when he opened it a distraught cat jumped out and ran round the room.

'We waited with baited breath for the expected carnage when one bright lad shouted: "Look sir, it's a black and white cat – it supports the jolly old Queens!"

"So it is, so it is," agreed Farmer, and class resumed without the anticipated summary executions.'

A TEACHER tells us she overheard a fifth-year pupil ask a classmate: 'How many ribs do you have?' When the boy answered: 'Three' the girl was surprised and told him: 'Three? I was thinking about twenty!' To which the boy told her: 'Oh, I thought you meant how many do I have for dinner.'

SURELY in Scotland of all places, people with red hair should not be getting a bad time? However a reader tells us that her sister had not been well after the birth of her child and had not been out much. Our reader says: 'So the first day she ventured out with the baby in the pram, a neighbour looked in it and said "Oh, he's got red hair, is that why you've not been going out?"'

OUR story of the wean with red hair makes reader Tom Bradshaw think he can delve into a very old joke-book and tell us: 'Overheard in Bellshill Main Street. "My, your wean's got a lovely heid of red hair. Does he take after his faither?" "Ah don't know, he never took his bunnet aff."'

WE mentioned Farmer Kelly at St Mungo's Academy, and Dave Hill recalls: 'He wasn't headmaster but head of History. He used to wear a deerstalker hat and a trench coat buttoned up to the neck with a sprig of heather pinned on it.

'At one point he belted all in my class (4A, 1957) who had failed the History exam, and then belted the rest of us who had passed, for cheating.'

SWIMMING baths continued. A reader tells us that some years ago a group of weans from a Drumchapel nursery school were taken to the baths for the first time. When they returned, one wee lad was asked how he'd enjoyed it. 'It was rubbish,' he replied. 'She dipped me in and oot like a teabag.'

IT was back to school for many Scottish schools. Alan Duncan tells us his grandson argued with his mother that he had been going to school for three years, and that was enough for him. Says Alan: 'My daughter-in-law gently explained he had to go back. If he didn't she would be taken away to jail for not sending him.

'To which he replied, "For how long?"'

WE must say adieu to the dodgy French translations, but not before Ned Keating in Michigan tells us: 'My late father, who taught French for many years had a favourite from the many he encountered in his career, 'Une longue suite de jours prospères' which a student rendered, not as 'a long series of successful days' but as 'a lounge suit that had seen better days'.

DEEDEE CUDDIHY tells us of the principal of Glasgow's College Of Commerce many years ago wanting action taken against students who were 'tagging' college walls by spraying their names on them. He amused his staff by then asking who this student Bob Marley was who seemed to be a persistent offender.

10
Famous Folk

Many Scots are not overawed by celebrity, but they will usually come away with a funny story if they meet someone well known.

ALEX FINDLAY in Kilmarnock swears to us that a friend of his aunt was in a hotel where the members of the band *Status Quo* were in the lobby. The aunt's friend couldn't stop herself from going up to singer Francis Rossi and saying she thought she knew him, but didn't know where from.

Trying to be helpful he told her: 'Rossi.' But she replied: 'No son, it can't be that. I've no' been to Rothesay for years.'

ROD STEWART opening the Glasgow Hydro reminds us of the story Scots author William McIlvanney told of meeting actor Sean Connery at a Scotland match at Hampden. 'I can't believe I'm here,' Connery tells him. 'I was sitting in Tramp's at two o'clock this morning when Rod Stewart walks in. He's chartered a private plane and why don't I come to the game. So, here I am.' Tramp's, of course, being a well known London nightclub. A policeman who was with McIlvanney chipped in: 'It's a small world, big yin. Ah was in a house at Muirhead at two o'clock this mornin'. It was full o' tramps as well.'

TALKING of McIlvanney, congratulations to him being presented with the Fletcher of Saltoun Award by the Saltire Society for his contribution to Scottish literature. His books about the Glasgow detective Laidlaw, which are streets ahead of most Glasgow detective literature, have been republished by Canongate. As McIllvanney modestly put it recently: 'What I don't know about Glasgow would fill several books. Some people might say it has.'

ILLEGAL postering. Musician Roy Gullane recounts: 'Back in the 1970s, a couple of friends were fly posting for a concert we were giving in the City Halls. They were apprehended by one of Glasgow's finest who, of course, wanted their names, which he was given. 'Occupation?' he further enquired. "Unemployed bill posters" the reply.'

MEETING celebrities continued. A Scots businessman tells us he and three other Scots were at the exclusive K Club golf club in County Kildare, Ireland, where they were a bit boisterous while sharing the bar afterwards with movie star Clint Eastwood. Eventually one of the Scots went over, and using Clint's classic *Dirty Harry* line, asked: 'Clint, could you make my day?' Clint replied: 'No. But you could sure make my day by shutting up.'

Only then did he relent and agree to a picture.

PAISLEY-BORN film actor Gerard Butler stars in the White House action film *Olympus Has Fallen*. A reader who saw the film the other night heard a fellow cinema-goer comment to his girlfriend as he left: 'So a guy frae Paisley stoats off at the end of the movie without the burd or the lead off the roof. Whit's the world comin' tae?'

ACTOR Rupert Everett, speaking at the Edinburgh Book Festival about his second volume of memoirs, *Vanished Years*, talked about his big break in Glasgow in the 1970s at the Citizens Theatre. Recalling the Glasgow audiences, Rupert said: 'Provided the play ended at 10:20 when the last bus left, the audience really enjoyed themselves. However, if the show ran on even a minute late, the audience would still get up at 10:20 – and you could hear the clatter, clatter, clatter of their seats as they left.'

CELEBRITY encounters continued. Guy Robertson, boss of Guy Robertson Advertising in Glasgow, tells us: 'I took a very proper lady from an Edinburgh law firm to a sports dinner and she was seated next to boxer Frank Bruno. As she had arrived after the formal introductions, I told her it was comedian Lenny Henry. She chatted away oblivious, then asked, 'Mr Henry, could you please do that *Know What I Mean 'Arry* impersonation of that thick boxer?' To his credit Frank just went ahead and did it. It was only later in the evening when the MC name-checked him that she realised.'

AND a chef in a leading Glasgow restaurant says he occasionally has fun with famous people by looking at them quizzically and asking: '*River City*?' 'The silence is usually deafening,' he tells us.

RETIRED *Herald* journalist Jack Webster tells in his just-published autobiography *A Final Grain of Truth*, of meeting Margaret Thatcher's husband Denis, who told him the tale of catching a train from St Pancras and sitting by mistake in a reserved carriage. Recalls Jack: 'It was the annual outing of a mental institution, said Denis, and when it filled up the lady superintendent began a head count. She went: "One, two, three, four", then came to Denis. "Who are you?" she asked. "I'm the husband of the Prime Minister."
The lady continued, "Five, six, seven."'

AMERICAN politician Hillary Clinton was at St Andrews University to receive an honorary degree. So, a group of students wrote inviting her to their housewarming party in the town's Queen's Gardens to give her a true feel for the town.

We like their explanation about party etiquette as their letter explains: 'We have officially stated that the party will begin at 9pm, although we would not at all be offended if you elected to arrive more around 10.30pm – everybody does that anyway, which is why we set the start time so early.'

Being students, the letter adds: 'BYOB'.

AFTER our story about Hillary Clinton, still being tipped as a future presidential candidate, coming to St Andrews, our political contact in New York phones to tell us: 'There is a new bumper sticker over here you can buy for your car. It says 'Run Hillary, run!' Democrats put it on the rear bumper and Republicans put it on the front bumper.'

READER Lenin the Parakeet – not his real name we suspect – e-mails to say he was in the chip shop next door to the old Apollo in Glasgow, standing beside the legendary jazz guitarist John McLaughlin who was appearing that evening. John was leaning over the counter and asking a member of staff slowly and incredulously: 'You FRY the pizza?'

WE mentioned schoolteacher turned politician Norman Buchan bringing protest singer Pete Seeger to Glasgow. Douglas Gordon tells us: 'I was assisting a friend, Ian Moonie, to fly post for a Seeger concert organised by Norman. We pasted the posters outside the Cosmo Cinema, and hurried to Norrie's locked van, and while he looked for the keys two policemen appeared. Ian lived in Partick and when asked his address replied: 'Dalcross Pass – pass as in Khyber.'

'The polis licked his pencil and asked "'ow do you spell Khyber?" We were later fined, and did not let Norrie forget this when he later had ministerial responsibility for the police.'

CELEBRITY encounters continued. David Speedie in New York recalls many years ago bumping into legendary baseball player and Marilyn Monroe husband Joe DiMaggio in an airport, who had a reputation for not giving autographs. Undaunted, David's wife went over and nervously blurted out: 'Mr DiMaggio, you're a great fan of my son.'

He found that so funny he immediately gave her the autograph.

FORMER *X Factor* winner James Arthur has fallen out with a few folk on Twitter, and posted: 'I wish I was still poor and unknown.'

'Give it a few months,' someone replied.

PHIL McCLUSKEY has just returned from a British tour with Texan duo *The O's* who were supporting *Del Amitri*. Phil says: 'One night the lads from Dallas were told that they would have to perform in front of the curtain. They had the 'great idea' of each walking from the side of the stage punching the curtain from behind before meeting in the middle where they would stick their heads through the gap. It was only later that night, driving back to the hotel, that one of them asked, "Hey Phil, who's Morcambe and Wise?"'

MIKE RITCHIE reads an interview with Loudon Wainwright III, a great hit in his last appearance at Glasgow Royal Concert Hall, in music magazine *Uncut*, in which the American singer/songwriter confesses that in his early twenties he would write songs that were about 'trying to get laid'.

But today he observes: 'Now when I say "come to my motel room", it's usually, "Can you show me how to work the WiFi?"'

THE BBC reported that the ceiling collapse at London's Apollo Theatre was caused by 'weak and old material being used'.

'Was Ken Dodd on stage?' asks a reader.

OUR story about the awkward conversations men have at urinals reminds a reader of Ian Macpherson, brother of Glasgow songwriter Bill Martin, standing in a loo while the chap further up whistled Eurovision winner *Puppet on a String*. Making conversation, Ian remarked: 'My brother wrote that.'

'Naw he didn't,' argued the fellow toilet user.

'Well he wrote the words,' said Ian, being more specific.

'Well I wiznae whistling the words,' replied the chap.

TRADITIONAL music group the *Tannahill Weavers* were playing their hometown of Paisley when band member Roy Gullane remarked to the audience that their thirty-two-year-old piper wasn't even born when they released their first album in the 1970s.

'Neither wiz his mammy,' shouted someone from the audience, casting aspersions on the good women of Paisley.

MAGICIAN Alan Hudson, appearing at the Gilded Balloon during the Edinburgh Festival, still remembers his first job on a ferry.

Alan says: 'It was my first night, and I asked someone what card they were thinking of and it would be the only card turned over in my deck. The first three guys I asked couldn't speak English.

'I finally found an English speaker who said "the three of Hearts" but when I went in to my pocket the deck wasn't there. I'd left it in the dressing room. When I returned with the deck and revealed the three of Hearts there was no applause. They all thought I turned it over in the dressing room.

'The cruise director made me do the bingo instead for the whole two months.'

ACTOR Simon Callow, who was at the Assembly Hall with his show *Juvenalia* during the Edinburgh Fringe, jumped into a black cab on his arrival in the capital. He had no doubt he was back in Edinburgh when he received the typical Fringe welcome from the driver, who turned round, looked at him, sighed and said: 'Oh, is it that time of year? Are you here again?'

TEXAN singer-songwriter Steve Earle appeared at the newly refurbished Kelvingrove Bandstand in Glasgow. Earle once said his mentor and friend, the late Townes Van Zandt, had given him a copy of *War and Peace* to read, which Earle dutifully did.

When he returned it to Van Zandt, he asked him when he had read it. Van Zandt replied: 'Hell, I haven't read it, I just thought that you should.'

MAKING her first appearance at the Fringe this year was writer and actress Davina Leonard with her play *Making It!* at the Assembly's George Square theatre. The show's main character, Jess, has a call with her mother, in which mum is not supportive of her daughter's acting career and keeps sending her advertisements for secretarial jobs. At a preview show, after Davina had left the stage and the audience started to clap, Davina's mother stood up, turned around to the full house and declared: 'I'm not really like that, by the way.'

T In The Park reminded us of a former colleague phoning a chart star, known for her experimental avant-garde electronic pop, for an interview before she appeared there. When the phone was answered he could hear a metallic whine subsiding in the background.

'Were you mixing tracks for your new album?' he asked, only to detect reproach and pity in her voice as she replied: 'No, I was hoovering my couch.'

JAKE LAMBERT tells us: 'Nobody can ever believe it when I tell them I once turned down Rihanna.' He then added: 'But then they don't realise just how loud my sister was playing her radio.'

AL MURRAY in his persona as 'The Pub Landlord' had a comedy gig recently in Glasgow. He likes Glasgow. As he told his fans: 'Glasgow: where I saw a junkie throw hot coffee in another's face while American tourists looked on.'

COMEDIAN Jim Davidson is returning for two night's at Glasgow's Pavilion Theatre. We remember when Jim appeared in pantomime at the Pavilion and popped into Nick's in the west-end for a beer. The barmaid asked a regular who he was and he told her it was Freddie Starr.

So, the next time she served Jim she said: 'My Mum wants to know if you really did eat that hamster?' Davidson, to be fair, exploded with laughter.

FORMER *Taggart* star Blythe Duff has won the Critics Award for her portrayal of a Glasgow gangster's daughter in the play *Ciara*. She once told her audience after appearing in the play at Glasgow's Citizens that because of the bad language and adult themes in the play, she told her two daughters: 'I've got to warn you about this new play I'm doing.'

'Oh my God, you're not taking your clothes off are you?' asked a worried daughter. When Blythe reassured them her clothes stayed on, they had no qualms at all about the bad language.

GLASGOW-BORN songwriter Bill Martin, awarded an MBE in the Queen's Birthday Honours, is wondering if he should have a quiet word with the Queen about royalties when he goes to Buckingham Palace. Bill penned the Cliff Richard hit *Congratulations*, which is frequently played by the Royal Marine band at Buck House events.

Says Bill: 'I bought the bandmaster a few whiskies before the royal baby was born and suggested he play *Congratulations*. After the fifth half, he told me I was wasting my money as the Queen had already requested it.'

CLAIRE HEALY, performing her cabaret *Playdough Face* at the Sweet Grassmarket during the Fringe, told us: 'As a joke, one song asks the question, "Have you ever eaten a goldfish for a bet?" No one says yes. Never. Nowhere. Except Dublin.

'One man revealed that, yes, he had eaten a goldfish. As the room turned to him in horror, he went into defensive mode. "I didn't eat the whole thing."'

A SOUTH-SIDE of Glasgow husband was on pick-up duty to collect his wife and daughter after the Dolly Parton show at the city's hydro. He phoned to ask when the show finished and was surprised it was earlier than he thought. When he queried the time he was told: 'It's because she's got no support.'

He couldn't stop himself from replying: 'Dolly Parton? Really?'

WHEN the Edinburgh Fringe brochure came out we bumped into Maxine Jones who was putting on her show *Invisible Women*, at The Merchants' Hall, about how women in their fifties seem to turn invisible and get overlooked. 'Though I do find I've slept with more people as I've got older,' Maxine tells us. 'On trains, planes, buses – I just can't stay awake,' she explains.

LACONIC former accountant Arnold Brown received a lifetime achievement award at the Scottish Comedy awards last night in Glasgow. Arnold is widely regarded as the godfather of alternative comedy. We liked Arnold's reaction to getting the award. 'It's always been great to be regarded as the comedian's comedian,' he said, 'but my real ambition has always been to be the bank manager's comedian.'

UNDERWEAR manufacturer Michelle Mone has divided folk into those who welcomed her posing in a swimsuit for a British Airways commercial, and others who think it is just another example of her seeking publicity.

We did like one chap who commented: 'On the whole I'm glad it's Michelle Mone promoting an airline, rather than Richard Branson promoting her brassieres.'

WE mentioned possible new songs for Paul Simon after the police were called to his house where he had allegedly been fighting with his wife. Actor Alex Norton contributes: 'Apparently as a way of saying sorry, Paul composed a song for his wife as the squad cars arrived – it's called the *Sound of Sirens*.'

TOM LAURITZEN reads in *The Herald* about the Aye Write! literary festival in Glasgow, and an appearance by Vicky Pryce 'who was sentenced to eight months in prison with her former husband', and he thought to himself, what a severe punishment.

MUCH debate about whistleblower Edward Snowden being elected Rector of Glasgow University. Journalist Iain Martin was recalling when he edited the *Glasgow University Guardian*, and singer Pat Kane was elected Rector. Kane offered to write a column for the *Guardian*, but Martin found the writing terribly pretentious. So, in the next column, Kane's reference to American futurist Alvin Toffler was changed to Alvin Stardust. It was the last column Kane offered them.

COMEDIAN John Bishop, who has appeared frequently on the TV show *Live at the Apollo*, is doing two nights at Glasgow's Hydro this year when he goes on tour. A reader, perhaps not a fan, phones the 'Diary': 'They say if you come from Liverpool you're either a musician or a comedian.

'John Bishop must be some musician then.'

NO more mentions of Chester Drawers, but we have a soft spot for Chic Murray of course, and Angus Johnston reminds us: 'You'll surely recall Chic Murray's monologue when he purported to be called Charlie Drawers? His father ran a drapery shop in partnership with an Islay man called Simmit.

'Simmit and Drawers, Drapers. His youngest brother was called Chester – he was a tall boy –a bit wooden. Father's advice when Chic was going out into the wide world: "Never let the Drawers down."'

AMERICAN country music singer Jace Everett, writer of the *True Blood* TV show theme tune, 'I Want To Do Bad Things To You', played at Glasgow's Òran Mór on Sunday night, but got lost walking to the venue from his hotel. He went up to a parked police car, explained who he was, and asked where he could get a taxi. Instead the cops told him to jump in and took him to the Byres Road venue. As Jace told the audience: 'First time I've been in the back of a cop car and I wasn't crying.'

Boyzone to play gig in Inverness

BOYZONE is the latest big name band to announce a Highland date.

The original Irish boy band, which has sold over 15 records worldwide, will appear at the Northern Meeting Park in Inverness on Saturday 27th August.

Former "X Factor" winner Shane Ward will provide the support for Boyzone in front of 12,000 people at the city centre venue.

MORE on meeting celebrities who can in fact be a tad modest. James Miller in Orkney was sitting in a Glasgow restaurant when he thought he spotted Robert Plant from one of the world's biggest selling bands *Led Zeppelin*. He asked the waiter who told him: 'Aye, it's him, right enough. He asked me if the restaurant was anywhere near to what used to be Green's Playhouse as "I used to play some music there."'

TALKING of celebrities, a reader heard a young woman discussing seeing a well known television star in Glasgow's Hilton Hotel. As she put it: 'As I glanced at him he gave me that 'Yeah, I know you know who I am' look. So, I gave him my best 'no idea' look, and went back to the bar.'

WE like the interview with Boothby Graffoe on the Glasgow comedy club The Stand's website in which he is asked about his show *Scratch!*, about lotteries and scratchcards, which is on in Glasgow. Asked: 'What research did you do?' he replied: 'I looked at the socio-economic effects of the lottery. It's disheartening when you realise that, despite the charitable benefits, there is a terrible greed underpinning the entire concept. With this show I'm hoping to make people see that if they win a lot of money then the greatest thing they could do with it is to help other people.'

'If you were to win big, would you continue with the tour?'

'You wouldn't see me for dust.'

SINGER Rod Stewart has just finished a great run of concerts at Glasgow's new Hydro. Alan Barlow in Paisley tells us of a previous trip by Rod to Glasgow when he stopped off at one of his favourite pubs, the Wee Barrel in Paisley, en route to Glasgow Airport.

Says Alan: 'Rod bought all the locals a drink. An old punter in the corner failed to recognise the blond troubadour but called over, "Thanks son. Did you have a wee win on the horses?"'

KEN McCLUSKEY of indie rock band *The Bluebells* was reminiscing about the time in the 1980s he missed band practice because he had seen one of the first salmon to return to the Clyde at Blantyre, and he rushed home to get his fishing rod. He was approached on the bank by two police officers who told him to move on as he did not have a fishing permit. The scene was caught by a *Herald* cameraman on the opposite bank and the story appeared as: 'First poacher caught on the Clyde for 100 years.'

SINGER James Blunt is not to everyone's taste, but he showed a nice line in humour on Twitter recently. When a fan tweeted: 'I must be one of only two who genuinely likes every James Blunt song. The other person being him.' He replied: 'Nope, you're on your own.'

When someone else posted: 'James Blunt just has an annoying face and a highly irritating voice,' the singer added:'And no mortgage.'

OUR story about the groom getting his marriage vows mixed up reminds a Troon reader: 'The late great Dave Allen told about being at his first burial as a child and hearing the priest give the final blessing. He was well into his teens before realising the words were not 'The Father, the Son and into hole he goes.''

JOHN FISHER's updated book on British comedians, *Funny Way to Be A Hero*, recounts how Edinburgh's Ronnie Corbett met his future stage partner Ronnie Barker when Corbett was working between jobs as a barman in a London club for actors. Because of his lack of inches there were two crates behind the bar, which he stood on, one with the name Agnes and the other with the name Champ.

It was only when Barker asked him who Agnes was that Corbett explained it was a crate marked Champagnes that had been sawn in half.

OUR mention of singer Rod Stewart stopping off in Paisley pub the Wee Barrel reminds a reader of one of Rod's first visits to the pub en route to Glasgow airport. He autographed one of the pub mirrors with a lipstick . . . and was told he would be barred if he did it again.

SINGER Susan Boyle appeared at the Clyde Auditorium, Glasgow, in a charity night for the Prince and Princess of Wales Hospice. We well remember after her sensational *Britain's Got Talent* appearance two smartly suited chaps were seen wandering around her home village of Blackburn, West Lothian. They went into a local pub where they asked the barmaid why the premises were so empty. When she asked where they were from, they said American television company CBS, wanting to do a piece on Susan.

'CBS!' she told them. 'We thought you were DSS, which is why everyone bailed.'

AMERICAN singing star Johnny Cash's visits to Glasgow still provoke memories. John Kelly in Baillieston tells us a friend was an usher in the old Green's Playhouse when Cash had two shows on the same day. John says: 'As the man in black entered from the wings he tripped on a trailing cable and drawled: 'Who put that darned thing thar' to much amusement.

'Ever the showman, Johnny decided to keep it in the act and amazingly tripped at the exact same spot at the second show that evening.'

CONGRATULATIONS to Glasgow-born John Lunn for winning an Emmy in America for his *Downton Abbey* music. John once explained that he wanted to play the cello at school in Stirlingshire but they were all taken – and he was given a double bass instead.

John added: 'So, few people played the instrument, and very quickly I was dragooned into playing for every orchestra in the county even though I could barely play it, so I was forced to learn very quickly.'

And from that decision, his musical career took off.

11
Shopping

Despite the rise in internet shopping, Scots still like the challenge of going out to the shops. This is what happened.

A READER was pushing a trolley around a south-side Asda when he heard two woman who bumped into each other chatting. 'I thought you normally go to Waitrose?' one of them asked. 'I do,' replied the other. 'But I couldn't go to Waitrose dressed like this.'

READER Debbie Meehan was using the Internet to read reviews of kettles before going out to buy one. She was reminded of the importance of grammar and punctuation when she read one review which stated: 'Within two years both my daughters and my kettle started leaking around the bottom seal so they had to be disposed of.'

A BEARSDEN reader tells us he was shopping with his wife, who wanted a dress for a wedding they were going to. When she came out of the changing room in an outfit and asked him what he thought, he knew the pitfalls. Wanting to get home, told her: 'It's great. It makes your waist look smaller and your legs longer.'

From behind a rack of dresses near him, a female voice called out: 'I want one of these. Where are they?'

NEWS that the Glasgow Barras market was to be smartened up before the Commonwealth Games reminds a reader of going there many years ago when a chap was trying to flog a vacuum cleaner and shouting: 'It'll cut your housework in half, missus.'

'I'll take two, then,' replied the woman he was directing his sales pitch at.

A READER in Glasgow's Sauchiehall Street heard a couple of women discussing a well known chemist's store with one declaring: 'I'm not going in there. There's always someone badgering me to buy their anti-ageing cream.'

'They never do that to me,' said her pal smugly.

'Must see you as a lost cause,' replied her friend crisply.

NICHOLAS WILSON tells us he saw a chap at a posh shop's fish counter who mistakenly pointed at quite a large plastic display lobster and said he wanted that one. Full marks to the assistant who didn't want to embarrass the chap and instead told him that the smaller lobsters were fresher.

SAD to see that Miller's art shop in Glasgow is facing closure. It has been a haven for the city's art students for generations. A former member of staff tells us that students frequently sent their mothers in at the start of term to buy their art supplies as A) it saved them getting out of bed and B) their mothers coughed up for the bill. One mother had such a lengthy list that she simply handed it over to a member of staff who read through it before shouting over to a colleague: 'Where do we keep the condoms?'

ANOTHER shopper at Miller's was gangland murderer Jimmy Boyle, who wrote his book *A Sense of Freedom* while in Barlinnie's Special Unit, where he took up art. While still in jail, he was taken to Miller's on day release with a prison officer to pick up supplies. A staff member asked him to sign a copy of his book, which she had with her, and she gushed: 'I bet you're always been asked to sign it.'

'Not where I'm staying, no,' replied Jimmy.

SOMEONE perhaps missing the point was the flustered chap seen by a reader in an Argyll café who ordered a vast range of snacks and drinks for his family sitting at a table behind him.

The girl serving him asked: 'Do you want a tray?' but he replied: 'Do you not think I've got enough to carry?'

JIM ANDERSON was passing the McDonald's branch in Inverness and noticed the company had printed 'Greasibh' on the door and initially thought it was a warning in Gaelic about the state of its products. Closer inspection showed that the company had actually put the slogan 'Greasibh air ais,' although Jim wonders if it would have been safer simply to stick to the English version 'Haste ye back'.

YOU still can't beat people in Ireland for being so lyrical in their conversations. A reader in a Dublin sandwich shop heard the girl behind the counter ask the elderly gentleman in front if he wanted feta cheese on his salad. 'Ah no thanks,' he told her. 'Feta cheese is a young man's game.'

A READER swears he was on the train to Dumbarton from Glasgow when a woman got on board with a couple of bags from a cheap and cheerful chain of stores. A pal she met asked if she had been shopping there and the woman replied: 'Yes. There was a story on the news about them using children in the Third World to make their clothes, so it seemed like a good cause to support.'

TENNENT Caledonian managing director John Gilligan was presented with the lifetime achievement award at the awards night in Glasgow of drinks industry magazine *Dram*. John recalled his early days as a salesman with Dryburgh, when the company introduced fuel cards for the salesmen's cars and people soon added on newspapers and soft drinks when buying their petrol at the garage.

Things came to a head, John said, when their boss called the reps in and asked: 'Right, who bought the barbecue?'

WE get inundated with these moneysaving offers sent to your email. Donald Grant in Paisley was looking at one from Groupon which promised him 'Mole or wart removal. 89% off' and he muses: 'Surely it would be better if they just removed the whole thing?'

A COLLEAGUE wanders over to interrupt us with the suggestion: 'Liven up trips to Tesco by mischievously dropping a pregnancy test into a couple's trolley.'

IAN SOMMERVILLE in Largs tells us: 'As a greetings card wholesaler we came across many slip-ups, including the card titled 'To my husband' which inside had the message 'Sorry you're leaving'.'

GERRY McCULLOCH was in a Largs store when he thought a young boy with his mother was being a tad pretentious when his mum asked him what he would like and he replied 'jamon' instead of merely saying 'ham.'

However Gerry had to quickly revise his thoughts on who was being pretentious when the mother replied without batting an eyelid: 'Serrano or Iberico?'

POSH folk in shops. Patricia Dunbar tells us about a lady from one of the more desirable enclaves on the south-side, who was shopping in the Laura Ashley store in Glasgow and remarked how hard work it was redecorating a room. Patricia says: 'The assistant empathised saying she had just finished painting and papering her bedroom herself and it was indeed hard work – and the lady had her work cut out before her. 'Good heavens!' replied the good lady of Newton Mearns, 'I just meant choosing the wallpaper, I don't do manual labour."

OUR mention of the chap struggling to buy a bra for his wife provoked entertainer Andy Cameron to take us back, we suspect, to the world of variety theatre, by telling us: 'A wee Glesga chap went into a ladies' lingerie shoap and asked for a bra for his wife. When the assistant asked what size he said, 'It must be a fifteen, hen'. Seeing the puzzled look on the assistant's face, he whipped off his bunnet and explained, 'Aye hen, this is a size seven and a hauf, and this fits wan o' them."

Goodness, we can almost feel a hook coming out from the side of the stage.

THE shopping site Amazon asks for reviews of products it sells and the company has revealed its favourites. It includes a run-of-the-mill roll of aluminium foil which led to one purchaser putting on the Amazon site: 'When I wrap my naked body in this lush, extravagant foil I feel transformed, and I wander the streets, mostly at night, fighting crime.'

OUR story of the fruit van in Glasgow with the sign stating that no bananas were left in it overnight reminds Angela Morgan of her company moving to a south-side industrial estate in Glasgow last year. Says Angela: 'On my first visit to the local shop I asked for a banana. This was greeted with a pause, raised eyebrow and the question, "What? A fresh one?" I didn't enquire about the eggs.'

A READER tells us how difficult it has become to order a cup of coffee these days. He was in a Glasgow cafe when a chap sat down and asked for a coffee. The girl rhymed off all the different types of coffee he could have but he interrupted her with: 'Just instant's fine.' and she told him: 'If you want instant coffee you'll have to wait.'

THE Barras market continued. George Ferguson in Castlecary remembers the chap selling lace curtains and tells us: 'He had a helper who would collect the money and distribute the purchased netting as the salesman cut off the measured length of material. As all the crowd held up their cash above their heads shouting, "I'll have ten yards" or "Eight yards for me" a typical wee wumman piped up with, "half a yard, please."

'Without pause for breath our hero's reply was, "Half a yard hen? Very good. Are you treating the budgie?"'

A READER in one of Sauchiehall Street's cheap and cheerful stores heard a woman shopper muse out loud as she held up some footwear: 'It's either the slippers or a McDonald's.'

A READER heard a woman on his bus ask her pal: 'did you see the picture of Prince William and Kate with baby George? He was wearing a jumper with his name on it.'

'Good to see,' said her pal, 'that they shop in Asda like the rest of us.'

TALKING posh continued. Linda Owens in Kirkintilloch recalls: 'Back in the 1950s, when door-to-door salesmen were common-place, my English mum opened the door to a man who said, 'Dae ye want a wundae cleaner?' Thinking the Glasgow gentleman was trying to sell her a vacuum cleaner made by a firm called Wonder, she replied, 'No thank you, we have a Goblin', which was a brand of cylinder vacuum. She observed his startled look and hasty depar-ture. Took her ages to work out that he was a window cleaner. She never saw him again.'

OUR tales of talking posh remind a reader of a new take on an old story. She tells us: 'I had a friend's wee boy over for dinner and served melon as the first course. He asked if I had any ginger.

"Irn-Bru or Coke,' I replied. He just looked at me and said, 'Cin-namon will do if you don't have any".'

AN Edinburgh reader swears to us she was in a supermarket in one of the more challenging areas of the city when she heard someone ask their partner: 'Shall we get these Monster Munch?' 'Are they buy one get one free?' 'Nah, half price,' was the reply. 'Nah,' said the companion, and they walked on.

A READER from Rhu was strolling in Helensburgh when he heard a brat, sorry, young child, whine to its mother: 'But why can't we go to Waitrose?' The mother replied: 'Because it's far too expensive.'

At that, the mum bumped into an acquaintance and after saying hello, turned to her child and said: 'We're just off to Waitrose, aren't we darling?'

BEN VERTH swears to us that he saw a middle-aged woman coming out of a charity shop in Edinburgh's Morningside, waving a pair of socks about, and calling back into the shop as a parting shot: 'It's just laziness! They're still a good pair if you gave them a wash and stitched the holes.'

DIETING is always difficult. A Milngavie reader tells us her pal was complaining that she had two eggs for breakfast. 'There's only 150 calories in an egg,' our reader told her.

'Not when they're Cadbury's,' her pal replied.

TALKING posh in shops, continued. Murdo Macdonald tells us that when Michael Munro's book of broad Glasgow humour, *The Patter*, was published, his pal Allen McCulloch heard a woman in a bookshop ask in a posh accent: 'Do you have that book on the Glasgow vernacular?'

A READER says: 'I overhead a chap in my local store during the sleet when offered a carrier bag for his newspaper said, 'No thanks. If it gets wet it can be dried over the radiator, then my man will iron it.' I think he was kidding, but in Helensburgh you never know.'

KENNETH STANTON remembers potatoes being sold off a lorry door-to-door. Says Kenneth: 'My mother, being a farmer's daughter, and thus familiar with various varieties of potatoes, asked the laddie what type they were. After a brief pause he replied, 'Raw yins, missus.''

ANDY JAMIESON in Bearsden worked a summer hols in the seventies with lemonade delivery firm Alpine and tells us: 'I chapped a door in Penilee and the wee girl who answered said they weren't needing any.

'Then a gruff old lady's voice pipes up from the back room: 'Two bottles of lime and a bottle of lemonade'. The wee girl insisted they didn't want any, but again comes the voice: 'Two bottles of lime and a bottle of lemonade'.

'Completely thrown, I said: 'But your granny wants some ginger'. She replied: 'Mister, that's the mynah bird', and slammed the door in my face.'

NOSTALGIA alert! As we were talking about home deliveries, Terry McGeary in East Kilbride goes way, way back and says: 'One of my gran's favourite stories was from her childhood when coal was sold around the streets from a horse and cart. She and her pals would run after the cart chanting, 'What do you feed your horse on?' awaiting the vendor's cry of 'Coal!', at which point they fell about helpless with laughter. Never failed to amuse apparently.'

DAVID DONALDSON recalls: 'Back in the seventies, when tins were still the norm and food was just beginning to get a bit trendy, we employed a lot of sewing machinists. I remember one of them announcing indignantly to all and sundry: 'I sent my wee girl to the shops for some spaghetti and what did they give her? Stiff spaghetti!''

OUR mix-up over spaghetti story reminds Ian Forrest in Laurencekirk: 'A woman my wife knows ordered a garment whose colour was described as cornflower. She was most indignant when it arrived and was blue, as she assumed it would be white like the cornflour she used in her kitchen.'

TALKING posh in shops: Eric Hudson in Bearsden says he was in a wee newsagents in town just before Christmas one year when he heard the posh woman in front of him ask: 'Do you have a copy of the *Browns' Book*, please?'

TALES of talking posh remind entertainer Andy Cameron of the classic yarn: 'An old friend of mine in Ru'glen had a date in the sixties with a rather posh girl who had attended Westbourne School for Girls, and he took her to The Bernie Inn. Struggling to find conversation, he thought he'd been rescued by a lady at the next table who collapsed. Boabby jumped up and declared to his date: "It's OK I've seen this afore, ah think she's jist havin' a wee epileptic foot."'

TALKING posh in shops, continued. Matt Vallance says: 'Many years ago, I was in Woolworth's in Ayr with my mother at the sweets counter. A well-groomed lady, quite obviously from Alloway, or perhaps Troon, was ahead of us and she, in a cut-glass voice, asked the lassie behind the counter for, "A bar of noo-gah please." Blank look from the shop assistant, until my mother stepped forward as interpreter. "The wumman wants nugget hen," brought a completion of the sale.'

MANY folk have been selling unwanted items on the Internet site *Gumtree*. Reader Kate Jackson had put up for sale a vintage hi-fi with turntable, tape deck and radio. She thought she had a buyer until he emailed via *Gumtree*: 'Thank you for your phone call. My wife overheard our conversation and said if I go about buying the hi-fi I would not be allowed back in the house, so sorry, cannot buy.'

BAKERY firm Greggs still has a strong hold on the eating regimes of many a west of Scotland chap. As reader Steve Fraser explains it: 'You stand in the queue admiring all the healthy salad options, low calorie juices, fruit, yoghurts, spring water, and when they shout 'Next!' for some unexplainable reason you spurt forth with "a steahhk bake, a packet ah cheese an' onion, an' a can ah Irn-Bru."'

AN EDINBURGH reader tells us: 'From the same people who add the warning to packets of roasted peanuts, 'Warning, may contain nuts' we now find the practice spreading to the clothing sector, with a Marks and Spencer label stating, '100% leather. Contains parts of animal origin.'

THE Guinness Book of Records has its own Twitter account. Someone sent to the Guinness people the pre-Christmas message: 'I've just seen someone completely smash the world record for 'Dithering around in a black Vauxhall Corsa in a Tesco car park.'

SOMEONE who perhaps over indulged his sweet tooth at Christmas was the colleague who emailed us: 'If you enjoyed Toblerone then you're really going to love Toblertwo.'

DAFT gag of the week. A reader says: '"Have you got a Barbie doll?" I asked the shop assistant. "You've got an interesting accent," she said. "It's a mixture of Australian and Scottish, isn't it?"'

OUR stories about the lack of religion at Christmas reminds David Martin: 'I was on a bus in Dundee and heard two girls catching up on Christmas presents. "My mum's got wee Joe an activity centre," one told the other. Obviously thinking of the Nativity scene, the other replied, "I didnae think yir mum wis religious," only to be reassured, "No, no the kind o' activity centre wi' the baby Jesus, the kind wi' hammers and things."'

SCOTLAND has slipped down the international league table of pupils being good at mathematics, according to news stories. A Newlands reader said it reminded her of being in a shop recently buying some items, which came to £12.74 and handing over a £20 note. When the assistant announced that there had been a power cut and that her till was not working so she could not work out the change, our reader told her: 'It's £7.26.'

'How do you know that?' asked the shop girl suspiciously.

12
The Law

Fortunately for most Scots, they are more likely to be on a jury than appear before one. Here is a peek behind the jury room door, and other tales of a legal nature.

A GLASGOW reader tells of being called for jury duty, and when she and her fourteen colleagues entered the jury room, a fellow jurist piped up: 'He looks so smart. I don't think he would do such a thing.'

A fellow member quickly pointed out to her that they had merely gone into the room to store their coats after hearing the indictment, and it was normal to wait until after they had heard the evidence before taking a decision.

ADRIAN WADDELL is reminded of kenspeckle Glasgow lawyer Len Murray's autobiography, *The Pleader*, in which he tells of a Dundee jury that found a chap guilty when many thought he would get off. Len wrote: 'The sheriff clerk asked one of the jurors what had led them to their verdict and was told by the juror that she had noticed the shoes of the solicitor for the accused were dirty. She had learnt never to trust a man with dirty shoes.'

WE asked for your jury service stories and a Merchant City reader tells us: 'The first thing we had to do was choose a foreman, so we quickly picked the guy who had gone to the toilet and told him when he returned.'

IAIN DUNCAN in Paisley tells us: 'Picked for jury duty in case of elderly Glasgow gentleman stabbed in the back by his wife – wounds were a series of jabs to the shoulder blade, and certainly not life threatening.

'The victim related that he was taken to Glasgow Royal Infirmary. The QC asked if he saw the doctor. "No" replied the victim. After a surprised look, the QC then said, "I'm led to believe that you did in fact see the doctor" to which the victim replied, "No, she was behind me."

'His wife was admonished and the old couple left hand in hand.'

PLANS to close the public counters in many police stations remind Robin Gilmour of the classic, that is, old, yarn of when Calderpark Zoo in Glasgow's east-end was shutting, and one of the lions in transit to a new home escaped.

Robin says: 'The story goes that three wee boys ran breathless into Easterhouse Police Station shouting, "Come quick – we've just seen the lion in Lochend Road."

'The officer, without lifting his head from his paperwork, replied: "Listen boys, I'm in here on my own. It'll just have to fend for itself."'

OUR tales of police stations remind a reader of Glasgow detective Joe Jackson's biography in which he told of John McVicar, before becoming head of CID, putting a fake dog poo on the station floor and pouring steaming hot tea on it for realism. The inspector arrived, threw a fit, told John to clear it up and was stunned when John picked up the offending item with his bare hands, before realising it was a joke.

The inspector thought it so funny he asked John to set it up for the divisional commander, who was visiting. John though, went to the kennel and brought back the real McCoy, which he placed on the floor. The commander came in, saw the poo, demanded it be cleaned up, and the smirking inspector bent down to pick it up.

ALTHOUGH not a police station story, a reader nevertheless is reminded of the miners' strike when picketing miners built a beautiful snowman at their picket line, which was destroyed when a police van reversed into it.

The next day the snowman was rebuilt but with a fake police helmet on its head. This appeared to annoy a police driver who then deliberately drove into it. The snag was the miners had rebuilt it over a metal traffic bollard.

RAYMOND HAINEY on the Royal Gazette in Bermuda tells us about a shoplifter in court who declared: 'I am Robin Hood. I steal from the rich and give to the needy.'

The magistrate merely replied: 'I'm the Sheriff of Nottingham. Thirty days.'

RETIRED cop Alan Barlow in Paisley recalled: 'When I worked in the old Greenock police office we had an admin inspector who looked after the stationery. He was searching the cabinets for an item and in one cabinet he found a cup of tea, drank it, and then continued his search without drawing breath.'

JURY duty continued. Says Brian Logan in Glasgow: 'After a four-day trial, we had found the defendant guilty by a unanimous decision. As we met for the last time and said goodbye to one another, I always remember one juror saying, "Cheerio then, I'm just away to fiddle my expenses."'

AS the search continues to find a site to replace Glasgow's Barlinnie Jail, we're reminded of Robert Jeffrey's book, *The Barlinnie Story*, in which he tells the classic tale of the newly appointed prison chaplain at the Bar-L who, peering at the mucky cup in which he was served tea, asked the trustee if the cup could get a good wash.

When the old lag brought the tray of tea into the meeting room, he inquired politely: 'Who wanted the clean cup?'

COMEDY writer Phil Differ's show about prison life, *Who's Afraid of the Big Bar-L*, being performed at Òran Mór during the West End festival, was previewed at Barlinnie, where the prisoners chatted to the performers afterwards. One prisoner interested in the production was asked if he himself had tried acting. 'Yes,' he replied. 'At Glasgow Sheriff Court. I wasn't very good.'

OUR story of the hospital kitchen workers playing late-night curling with frozen chickens reminds a reader of when he was a heating engineer employed on a project at Barlinnie Prison in Glasgow. 'It was night and we had access to the kitchens where we found a whole salmon in the freezer which we used as a bat in a game of cricket.

'The salmon was later pride of place a few days later at a dinner the Governor gave for honoured guests.'

TALKING of police, Joe O'Neill in Carluke tells us of a friend driving down south who was stopped at a random vehicle checkpoint where the suspicious police officer going round the van checking tyres and so on, spotted a leather pouch in the passenger door storage bin and asked what was in it. 'Binoculars,' replied the driver.

'What do you use them for?' asked the officer, and although it led to his entire van being searched, Joe's pal couldn't resist replying: 'To see things that are far away.'

OUR story recalling Paul McCartney's Campbeltown court appearance on a cannabis charge reminds Kate Woods that although the story was front page news in national papers, the local *Dunoon Standard* had it buried among the list of petty crimes under 'Court Reports'. Kate says: 'McCartney, described in the report as a musician, was apparently not personally known to Willie Ingles, the editor/owner of the *Standard* at that time, nor was he local, and therefore did not rate any special coverage.'

OUR tale of Paul McCartney's drug conviction reminds former *Daily Record* chief reporter Gordon Airs of checking in at a Campbeltown hotel to cover the case at the local sheriff court. The hotel owner got quite excited at the media interest and asked if a well known *Daily Express* reporter would also be attending.

'Why, are you a fan?' asked Gordon. 'No, he owes me money,' replied the hotelier.

FORMER police officer Gerry MacKenzie recalls a Glasgow Sheriff Court case where a bookshop in Glasgow had been raided and cine reel films of pornographic movies – this was before the days of DVDs – were seized.

The court collapsed in mirth when one of the films was being shown to the jury, and it was only discovered at the end that it was being shown backwards.

The clue was when the cast started yanking their clothes on and walking backwards out of the door.

13
Transport

Getting a train or a bus is when most people bump up against strangers with a story to tell. Fortunately, they then passed them on to the 'Diary'.

READER Robert White, from Kirkcudbright, was on a late night bus in Glasgow when two women came on, slightly unsteady, but still carrying shopping bags. Robert says: 'The bus stopped sharply and one of them yelled, "Ma tomatas are rollin' doon the bus." Her shopping bag had spilled. I picked up two tomatoes and said, "They're a wee bit bruised and dirty. You'll not be able to eat them now." "Och son. That's okay. They're no fur me. They're ma man's. He'll no ken they've been rattling aboot the bus."'

A READER was on a bus in Paisley when the hesitant driver announced he was taking his time as it was his first day on the route.

An elderly chap sitting near the front shouted out: 'I can show you a short-cut if you like.'

ROY INGRAM in Bearsden tells us of his friend travelling down to Glasgow from Aberdeen by train and sitting opposite two women who were joining a hen party, and who proceeded to drink two bottles of Buckfast before falling asleep.

Roy says: 'They were still asleep when the train arrived in Glasgow, so he nudged one of them awake and told her that the train had reached its destination. "Thanks," she said, "are you going to Stirling as well?"'

OUR train tales remind John Crawford of travelling from Glasgow to London overnight on Paisley Fair Friday when a well-dressed and well-refreshed businessman came on board, threw away the ticket from a reserved seat, sat down and began to sing 'The Song Of The Clyde' before falling asleep.

John says: 'He only woke to dodge the ticket collector during the night. When we arrived at Euston he disappeared again but came up to us on the platform to ask, "Did you folks notice if I had any luggage when I got on last night?"'

ALISON RUSSELL was waiting on the BA flight to Glasgow from Gatwick when the public address system seemed to announce: 'Would passengers not flying to Glasgow make themselves known to the desk.' Pandemonium all round as folk tried to check whether they were at the right gate, and people for other flights wondered if they had to go forward. Alison says: 'Realising his colleague might not have been speaking with the correct clarity, another member of staff tried again, slowly enunciating 'passenger Knotts' so that a rather sheepish young Mr Knotts made his way to the desk.'

OUR sleeping on the train story reminds Alastair Macpherson of the Aberdeen University student who used to travel by train to his home in Keith every Friday evening. Alastair says: 'Unfortunately, he often fell asleep and didn't wake up until the train reached the end of the line in Inverness.

'So he wrote 'Keith' on a large piece of cardboard and hung it round his neck before dozing off as usual. Imagine his chagrin when a member of the train staff woke him up, telling him, 'Hello, Keith. You'll be delighted to know that you are now safely in Inverness.'

THINGS you didn't know ... Donald Macdonald was on one of the new Edinburgh trams when the conductor explained that the people who stand about tram spotting are know as tram-oraks.

BBC news reported that two Ryanair jets collided on the ground at Stansted Airport and there was a three-hour delay before passengers were put on alternative planes.

'It took that amount of time for the passengers to cough up the fee for transferring to a different flight,' says a reader.

PILOTS continued. A retired sports journalist tells us about accompanying an Old Firm team to Eastern Europe when the chatty pilot on the chartered plane announced he wouldn't be at the game himself as he and his co-pilot were taking the two stewardesses out for dinner.

On the flight back to Glasgow following a nil-all draw, the pilot came on to tell the team: 'Sorry about the result. If it's any consolation, we didn't score either.'

INEVITABLY the press were waiting to report the first accident involving the new Edinburgh tram. As Gordon Beveridge in Wick tells us: 'Good to see that the young girl hit by a tram in Edinburgh was able to walk away afterwards without needing medical attention.

'So only mildly tramatised then.'

BRILLIANT weather in Glasgow, but certain standards are still kept. A reader watched as a young chap with his 'tap aff' in the sunshine boarded a FirstBus in the city centre.

However, after a quick conversation with the driver the young chap jumped off the bus, fished his t-shirt out of a plastic bag, put it on, and jumped back on the bus. 'Who knew,' said our reader, 'that Glasgow buses have a dress code.'

RICHARD Fowler was waiting for the Ardrossan to Kilmarnock bus the other day, which advertises a bus every eight minutes, but after waiting a quarter of an hour he expressed dissatisfaction to a fellow would-be passenger. The chap explained to him: 'They've a new rule at the Ardrossan terminus – they roll a dice and they need a six to start.'

A READER catching the bus into Glasgow is still puzzling over the woman he heard telling her pal: 'You know Marjory, and how she talks really fast? I've never heard anyone talk as fast as Marjory does.

'Her mother was just the same.'

GLASGOW'S old sludge boats which carried human waste out to sea, were being discussed at Jim Morrison's bowling club, where one worthy said he had worked on the SS Dalmarnock in the nineties. 'Was it not a bit smelly?' he was asked.

'A bit, at times,' he replied. 'But it was a great wee number, down the Clyde in the morning, back up in the afternoon, and for some reason I always got a seat to masel going home on the bus at night.'

YES, you might have a tram running in Edinburgh now, but you still can't beat the Edinburgh buses for interesting conversations. A reader was on Edinburgh's No.24 bus when he heard the girl in front of him tell her pal: 'I'm looking for a new place. I can't live with her anymore, she's such a slob. The other day we'd ran out of milk so she just dumped two of my Actimels in her tea instead.'

But her pal replied: 'At least she's a healthy slob.'

CATCHING the bus into Glasgow, a reader heard a young chap ask a pal he met: 'You look rough. Did you have one of your famous drunken nights?' 'No,' replied the pal. 'Sadly it was one of my not-so-famous sober nights.'

STRESSFUL places, airports. An Edinburgh Airport duty manager admitted that the new boarding pass security scanners occasionally cause confusion. 'Where it says facedown,' he says, 'we've even had people put their faces against the reader.'

A READER on the bus into Glasgow heard a young chap discuss with a pal a visit to a city centre club at the weekend.

'A girl at the bar asked me if I thought she had too much make-up on,' he recounted.

'I told her it depends on whether she was wanting to kill Batman or not.'

PENSIONERS love their free bus journeys. A south-side reader was behind two capering pensioners who were standing at the open door of a bus allowing each other to get on the vehicle before the other one.

Eventually one gestured the other forward and said: 'As I always say, age before beauty.'

Our reader heard the impatient bus driver mutter behind his screen: 'And as I always say, would someone get on the bloody bus.'

IAN BARNETT was shopping in the upmarket Fortnum & Mason's store in London as he had promised to bring his wife back some coloured sugar.

He asked the assistant to bubble wrap it to put in his suitcase as he wasn't sure he could carry it as hand luggage. Making light of it he joked with the assistant: 'I don't know why I am asking you to wrap this – how could I use a bag of sugar as a weapon on a plane?' 'The pilot might be diabetic, sir,' replied the assistant.

A READER says he could sympathise with the young girl on his train into Glasgow yesterday who told her pal: 'Nothing ruins your Friday like realising it's only Thursday.'

SOME people, observed a reader, take their animals far too seriously. He was on a train on the south-side when heard a woman tell her pal: 'I'm a bit worried – I told the dogs I'd be home over an hour ago – and you know how vindictive they can be.'

WILLIAM McKINLAY tells us of a business associate who was flying from Amsterdam to Glasgow for a meeting, only for the airline to lose his luggage. He was given a modest sum by the airline so that he could buy a replacement suit, but when he visited a Glasgow menswear shop and explained how much he had, the Glasgow assistant told him: 'I couldn't cover you in brown paper for that money.'

OUR mention of pilots' conversations reminds Alastair Bale in Giffnock of the retired captain who told him of once taking off from a coastal airport, and at about 16,000 feet remarking to his first officer: 'That ship down there is hove to.'
  To which the first officer replied: 'Good grief, can you read that from here?'

PILOTS continued. Tom Graham in Barassie says: 'Flying from Edinburgh to Norwich, I declined the stewardess's offer of a drink. Changing my mind later, I stopped her as she was passing and said

I would have a lager. She instantly handed me the one she was carrying saying, "Have this one. I'll get another for the pilot."'

OUR mention of airline pilots' pronouncements reminds Patricia Watson: 'I had a colleague whose husband was a pilot with Loganair. He said that one of the captains used to say, 'We apologise for the delay. The machine used to remove the handles from your luggage has broken down and the baggage handlers have had to do it manually.'

MY colleague Tom Shields always had a list of rules when flying with Ryanair, including 'Don't speak until you're spoken to.' I was reminded of this when Edinburgh reader Peter Henry told 'The Diary': 'I was boarding a Ryanair flight from Edinburgh to Faro, and thought I might have a bit of banter with the air hostess as I entered the plane:'Any chance of an upgrade?' I inquired.

'Try another airline,' came the swift response.

OUR story of the about-to-be-nationalised Prestwick Airport reminds Roy Gullane of flying into the Ayrshire airport from Canada some time ago when the hallway was lined with portraits of famous Scots. Roy says: 'The entire queue burst into laughter when it heard an American lady shouting to her husband, "Honey. What's a Bruce?"'

TALKING of buses, a reader was travelling on one into Glasgow when a young chap took out a sandwich and his hungry pal asked if he could have a bite. 'No,' said his pal, 'friendship and food – two very different things.'

AN Internet review of Prestwick airport, which Ryanair calls Glasgow Prestwick Airport, revealed: 'Got off the plane with some Eastern Europeans who got outside the terminal and remarked that they didn't expect Glasgow to be so rural.'

THE Glasgow banter . . . the driver of an early evening bus on Maryhill Road announced to passengers that, because it was quiet, he would perform a guided tour for their illumination. 'They big widden things on your left,' he announced. 'They're trees. The green stuff on the grun is grass.

'See that fire station on your left – that's where pole-dancing started in Glesca.'

Thus ended the brief but educational commentary.

SO, Prestwick airport is being bought by the Scottish Government. We remember the reader who flew in there and was standing behind a Japanese tourist at the restaurant who was pointing at the sausages. 'Mash?' asked the buxom Ayrshire lass serving. As he looked confused she said louder: 'D'ye want mash wi' that?' As this didn't seem to help, she elucidated: 'Mash, ye ken, tatties, mashed tatties.' At that point the young man took his sausages and fled.

HUMOUR on the London Underground, where a reader down on business was using the Tube at a busy time of day and heard a member of staff shouting: 'Keep left!' He thought it was quite sharp of the young chap who shouted back: 'Who's Keep?'

YES, it's that time of year. Reader Anne Alexander was woken at three in the morning on Saturday by a Glasgow punter on the phone who demanded: 'Can a huv a taxi fur 55 Mitchell Street?' Keeping her temper, Anne replied: 'Sorry, you've got the wrong number.'

The chap tested Anne's patience further by replying: 'Naw ah huvn'y – it's definitely 55 Mitchell Street.'

GLASGOW taxi drivers – still charmers on occasion. A reader in Springburn at the weekend was meeting her friends in town, and her taxi was waiting outside. Eventually she rushed down, climbed inside, and told the driver: 'I'm really late.' The chap looked at her in all her finery and replied: 'You're probably worth the wait,' which cheered her up no end.

PILOTS continued. David Muirie says: 'Following your piece about automatic landing systems, I recall being on a BA flight from Heathrow to Glasgow on a filthy night and had a very bumpy landing. The pilot came on the PA system and advised that the landing had been completely automatic.

'Behind me were two stewardess, one of whom said to the other, "no way was he going to admit that was one of his own."'

MEANWHILE for those getting out of Scotland at the weekend, a reader on the East Coast line tells us the morning announcement on his train could only happen in Scotland, he imagined.

A member of staff on board told travellers over the public address system: 'We have a range of alcoholic drinks on sale. I know it's a bit early, but why not start now?'

READER Frank Murphy tells us about a Glasgow taxi driver who picked up a tipsy female in town after a night out. She never spoke on the journey home until they arrived and she said: 'Can I ask how the fare is £9 when it was only £2 on the way in?' The puzzled driver argued: 'Couldn't have been £2. The meter starts at £2.40.'

'I'm telling you it was £2 each,' the girl insisted.

'Each?' replied the driver. 'How many of you were there?' 'Five.'

OUR tales of Glasgow's sludge boats remind Stuart Yeamans: 'When I was third mate on a general cargo ship, a great deal of time was taken up trying to prevent pilfering during loading or discharging operations. A friend of mine working on the sludge boats said that they never had that problem.'

14

No Longer With Us

Herald **readers remember some of the folk who passed away in the last year.**

THE death of Labour veteran Tony Benn reminds us of his visit to Celtic Connections in Glasgow when he told the tale of driving near Westminster many years ago and urgently needing to go to the loo. In desperation, he lifted the car's bonnet and relieved himself against the engine, hoping he would be out of sight. However a passer-by stopped him and said: 'I see your problem – your radiator's leaking.'

And when Tony spoke at the Mitchell Theatre in Glasgow on the fortieth anniversary of the UCS shipyard occupation, his contract stipulated, not the usual request for exotic vodkas, flowers or Smarties with the blue ones removed, but simply a cheese sandwich and a cup of tea.

APOLOGIES if you have heard this, but it would be remiss in not marking the sad passing of Lanarkshire singer Jack Alexander of Alexander Brothers fame without repeating the oft-told tale of the brothers arriving for a tour of Canada and being asked at Canadian passport control where they were from. 'Cam'nethan,' said Jack, only to be interrupted by Tom, who said: 'Ach, Jack, he'll no' know where Cambusnethan is,' and turning to the officer, announced: 'Wishae.'

THE death of hard-living singer/songwriter Lou Reed reminds us of seeing him at the Glasgow Apollo in the early 1970s. Lou looked a bit delicate, and legend had it that he had to be dragged from the car taking him to the Apollo semi-comatose. At one point he sat on the edge of the stage, which had a vertiginous drop to the audience. It was the only time we recall the Apollo bouncers turning their backs on the crowd and watching the act instead, in case they had to jump in to save him.

ALAN BARLOW was chatting to a barmaid in Paisley who said she once worked in a Paisley pub that catered many funeral teas. Alan says: 'These events were noted in the pub diary under the heading 'Purvey/Funeral'.

'A new barmaid started and was leafing through the diary when she opined that it was an awful shame that the Purvey family had lost so many of its members.'

SAD to hear of the death of Real Madrid legend Alfredo di Stefano. He will be especially missed by Celtic fans as di Stefano asked the Lisbon Lions to play in his testimonial game, watched by more than 100,000 fans in 1967. Jim Craig recalled in his book *Celtic Pride and Passion* that the day after the game in Madrid Jimmy Johnstone came down to the hotel reception with his wife Agnes and asked for a taxi.

When it arrived Jimmy got in the back and told the driver: 'Benidorm.' Recalled Jim: 'The look on the driver's face was one I will never forget. Madrid to Benidorm is around 230 miles, but for Jimmy, anything was better than flying.'

THE great investigative reporter Chapman Pincher has died at the age of 100. In his recent autobiography, Chapman wrote about his love of fishing in Scotland and revealed: 'Scottish ghillies are a breed unto themselves. I have a vivid memory of my ghillie shouting across the Dee to ask another why the owner of the beat and his guest were not fishing that day. The old man's yell, "They're awa tae Edinburgh on a drinking and whoooooring expedition" reverberated over the water.'

WE mentioned superstitions, and one of the most poignant in Deedee Cuddihy's book, *Scottish Superstitions*, was the chap who told her: 'My grannie went to the bingo in Partick almost every day and she always borrowed a rabbit's foot brooch of my mother's and laid it on top of her cards to bring her luck. And she was quite lucky. When my mother died I showed the brooch to a friend who said, "That's not a rabbit's foot, it's a grouse claw."'

SAD to hear of the death of doughty QC Jock Thomson, who was a well-liked figure in the Scottish courts. We recall when he was a young procurator fiscal in Glasgow prosecuting a chap selling blue movies. A sample film was being shown to the jury, which involved a couple who were accompanied on screen by a pig. The jury were eventually becoming bored with the movie as one jury member was heard to mutter: 'Has naebody telt them it's mare fun wi'oot the pig?'

TALKING of anniversaries, the media was asking everyone where they were when President Kennedy was assassinated fifty years ago, with the assumption everyone knew what an earth-shattering event it was. However one accountant in Glasgow tells us: 'I was at the Lifeboys that Friday evening, and I thought the officer's announcement "Bad news" meant the next day's fitba was cancelled.'

FOOTBALL fans will be saddened by the death of Bobby Collins, the Scotland and Celtic star who went on to become a great player for both Everton and Leeds. Showing it was a different era in the 1950s, a south-side reader who lived near Bobby, known as The Wee Barra, once explained: 'I drove a Pollokshaws Co-op bread van, and often gave Bobby a lift to Celtic's home games. No Porsches or BMWs for the players then.'

PROTEST singer Pete Seeger who has died, visited Glasgow a few times, often as a guest of Labour politicians Norman and Janey Buchan. Reader Paul O'Sullivan tells us that the biography of fellow performer Ramblin' Jack Elliott told of Pete and Jack appearing at Glasgow University, and beforehand Pete tried to rescue a log from the River Kelvin to use as a prop in an axe-chopping work song – and fell in.

Says the biography: 'With the concert less than an hour away, Seeger was spirited away to the hall by a sympathetic cabbie, but forced to perform that night in Jack's dry, but awfully tight-fitting shoes.'

JIMMY ELLIS, Bert Lynch on TV's *Z-Cars*, has sadly died. Jimmy worked on the show with director John McGrath who went on to start the 7:84 Theatre Company. When Jimmy's character was promoted to inspector he was told to go to a police function and hang out with an inspector to see how he acted. Jimmy recalled: 'When I left at 3am, he was standing on a table with his trousers around his ankles, playing an accordion with a pint balanced on his head, singing *Eskimo Nell*. So, I said, "that's how I'll play him."'

SANDY JARDINE was an utter gentleman, and the death of the Rangers great is a sad loss. We liked his explanation of his name Sandy. Although christened William Jardine, when he arrived at Ibrox a member of staff looked at his hair colour and said: 'Hey Sandy!' He knew the name had stuck when he was signing autographs for boys hanging about outside Ibrox with 'Billy Jardine' but the lads would look at it and ask suspiciously: 'I thought your name was Sandy?' 'It wasn't worth fighting,' said Sandy, and he changed his autograph.

THE film actor Bob Hoskins has died after an impressive career, often playing Cockneys and gangsters. We liked his question and answer interview with a newspaper when he was asked: 'Who would play you in the film of your life?' 'Danny Devito,' he replied. The next question was: 'What's the worst thing anyone's said to you?' 'Aren't you Danny Devito?' said Bob.

OUR tales of the late actor Bob Hoskins remind writer Meg Henderson: 'I had arranged to meet Sue Townsend in the Groucho Club and was searching everywhere for her. I went into the bar and Bob Hoskins asked if I was looking for Sue and I barked that I was. He said she'd left a message that if a disgruntled Scots female turned up to meet her he should tell her to pull up a pew and buy her a drink because she had wandered off, but would be back.

'I said I didn't drink and he said, "Jesus Christ, so that's the happiest you ever are?"'

SAD to hear of the death of comedy actor Rik Mayall, who was still in his fifties. Arguably his best role was as the amoral and devious Conservative politician Alan B'Stard in *The New Statesman*. The show's producer John Bartlett was once asked if it was time for a sequel and he replied: 'There was a sequel to Alan B'Stard. It was called Tony Blair, but it wasn't quite as believable and certainly not as funny.'

Incidentally, Rik felt the need to start a Twitter account over four years ago, and his first tweet was: 'Opening my very own Twitter to stop anyone else using my name. But don't expect to hear from me any time soon. Love Rik.' True to his word, despite having over 30,000 followers on Twitter, he never wrote another thing.

WE mentioned the sad death of comedy performer Rik Mayall, and reader John Dunlop recalls his company's seventy-fifth anniversary, when a steam train was hired to take the staff to Chester – and much imbibing of alcohol en route ensued.

Adds John: 'During the dinner after we arrived, Rik performed his outrageous slapstick comedy act, *The Dangerous Brothers* with Ade Edmondson.

'Our bemused managing director assumed they were just drunks off the train.'

SAD to hear of the death of the great black American writer Maya Angelou. Literary editor Rosemary Goring tells us that Maya was happy to put herself down when telling a story. 'There was the day,' says Rosemary, 'when she waited interminably to be served breakfast in an airport in North Carolina. Perceiving this as a racist slight, she summoned the waitress and told her that if there was a problem with serving her because she was black, she'd better tell her 'and then call the police.' The girl explained cheerfully that the chef had run out of grits and couldn't serve breakfast without them. She predicted the meal would be ready in 10 minutes. Maya said she felt "the ninny of all times."'

THE death of boxing promoter Mickey Duff reminds us of when he brought Muhammad Ali to Paisley ice rink for an exhibition bout – yes, hard to believe, isn't it? Anyway the story was told that during a dinner in Glasgow, Ali was introduced to Rangers star Willie Henderson, and seeing the footballer's lived-in coupon, Ali is quoted as telling Willie: 'Football! I'm glad I stuck to boxing.'

SAD to hear of the death of TV chef Clarissa Dickson Wright. We recall Clarissa, a terrible drunk for many years before joining AA, explaining that she once punched a policeman when she was drunk-driving a car as she thought that if she was arrested for that, she wouldn't then be breathalysed over her driving. Said Clarissa: 'The policeman, with a swelling black eye, asked me what he should tell his wife. I replied, "Say it was another woman," which he found so funny that he didn't charge me with the assault.'

TAKE *The High Road* and *Balamory* actress Mary Riggans has died at the age of seventy-eight. Former *Taggart* star Colin McCredie fondly recalls that Mary always used to call her admirers 'Herooties.' This was because whenever they spotted Mary in the street, they would cry: 'There's her oot ae *Take the High Road*!'

AS ithers see us. A reader sends us a gag from an English web-page: 'Edinburgh man Wullie McTavish is on his deathbed, knows the end is near, is with the nurse, his wife, his daughter and two sons.

'"Bernie," he says, "I want you to take the Braid Hills houses. Sybil, take the flats over in Morningside and Bruntsfield. Tam, I want you to take the offices in Charlotte Square. Sarah, my dear wife, please take all the residential buildings in the New Town."

'The nurse is just blown away by all this, and as Wullie slips away, she says, "Mrs McTavish, your husband must have been such a hard working man to have accumulated all that property."

'"Property? The eedjit had a paper round."'

MORE on the Kennedy assassination anniversary. Our contact in the world of traditional music says the late singer Calum Kennedy was often late paying musicians who accompanied him. He continued: 'The *Calum Kennedy Show* was on its annual Highland tour and were in Thurso that fateful Friday night. While Calum dined in the restaurant of the Pentland Hotel, the *Will Starr Band*

and the rest of the cast were eating in the hotel bar when a local rushed in. "Lads, have you heard? Kennedy's been shot!" The band's drummer, Billy Thom, slammed down his pint. "Oh goodness, we'll never get paid now."

That's the way Billy used to tell it, anyway . . .'

15
Youth

Young people can often see life differently from their elders.

AH the joys of youth. Ellen Crawford was out walking in Glasgow when a young chap came towards her on a bike. He stopped, pointed to where he had come from, and asked her: 'Are you going that way?' When Ellen answered in the affirmative, he proudly replied: 'Good – you'll see ma skid.'

A READER waiting for a bus in Glasgow's city centre heard an older chap tell a young woman puffing on a fag: 'That's a terrible habit.'

Barely glancing at him the girl replied: 'So's being rude to strangers.'

CONGRATULATIONS to Glasgow's Larry Dean for winning the Scottish Comedian of the Year contest. We liked the story Larry once told of sitting his mum and dad down in the kitchen and telling them he was gay.

'My father stormed out of the room,' recalled Larry. 'I was

standing there thinking I had ruined the family and how would we recover from this when he came back in and handed my mum a tenner.'

A DOTING grandfather in Milngavie watched his grandson wrestle with a cough bottle, unable to unscrew the cap before Grandad told him: 'It's childproof. Children can't open it.'

'How does it know I'm a child?' was the not-unreasonable reply.

A SOUTH-SIDE reader tells us she had her two young grandsons staying over at Easter while their parents had a break. She had put the boys to bed, and had gone for a shower when she heard them noisily jumping around the room. With her make-up off, clad in a dressing gown, and her hair bundled into a towel, she stormed into their room and told them to get to sleep. As she left the room she heard one of the boys whisper: 'Who was that?'

PROBLEMS we never realised existed. A reader tells us his teenage daughter recently took a job in a call centre, and when he asked her how the job was going she told him: 'A caller really made it difficult for me today. I asked him when his credit card expired and he said, 'April next year.' Do you know how long it took me to work out that I had to type in '04/15'?'

WE mentioned students not trying all that hard for jobs this summer. A reader swears to us he tried to encourage his daughter by reading out a newspaper advertisement where a local pensioner was looking for someone to do some light housekeeping. His daughter quickly replied that she didn't know anything about lighthouses.

A GLASGOW reader tells us about her group of girlfriends meeting up. One of them, a mother of four, was asked if she had her time again, would she still have four children? 'Absolutely,' she replied. 'Just not the same ones.'

A CHAP in a Glasgow pub was being asked how his teenage son was. 'It's the golden year,' he replied.

'What's that?' he was asked. 'It's the year when he's old enough not to need a babysitter, but too young to borrow my car,' he replied.

ARTIST Moose Allain tells us: 'My wife said the kids need to let off steam. So, I've got them bleeding the radiators.'

A READER on a train into Glasgow was amused by the teenage lad sitting opposite who told his pal: 'I couldn't find my phone this morning and my mum said, 'You can't really care for it if you lose it so easily'. So, I reminded her about the time she lost me in Tesco.'

ROBERT WHITE heard a little girl in Dumfries tell her mum: 'I feel sorry for Papa. He sits on his own with no-one to talk to except his dog, and nothing to do but watch TV. He's lonely and it's a shame.' The girl's mum replied: 'Would you like to spend some time with Papa this afternoon?' 'Nah,' said the little girl. 'Can we go for hot chocolate?'

CHILDREN SHOULD BE CAREFULLY OVERLOOKED BY PARENTS

Thank You

LOVELY day in Glasgow, with temperatures soaring and the sun shining. One reader at the Fort shopping centre heard an angry mother tell her whining young child: 'See that big yellow thing in the sky? The earth revolves around it, no' around you!'

'MY son wanted to know where the sun went at night,' a Kelvinside reader phones to tell us. 'So, I told him to sit up all night and he'd find out. It finally dawned on him at about half four this morning.'

A READER watched as a young man on Byres Road gingerly touched his hair then told his pal: 'Is there a more tense moment than the one after a drop falls on your head, and before you've checked it's water?'

'HAVE you ever taken part in any extreme sports?' a chap asked his pals in a Glasgow pub the other night.

After thinking about this, one pal replied: 'I did take my teenage daughter out for a driving lesson.'

HALLOWE'EN of course last week and Andy Cumming was on a Glasgow train when a Zombie showed the ticket inspector his rail pass. 'How do I know this is you?' asked the suspicious ticket chap.

AFTER our tale of the father suggesting Pancetta as a name for his baby, Peter Farmer in Johnstone swears to us: 'A female in a Kilbirnie supermarket was heard expounding, to all and sundry, that, she 'wiz gaun tae ca' hur wean Chlamydia.''

FUNNY how the meaning of words changes over the generations. A Newton Mearns grandfather was recalling his schooldays to the family, and told of the boy in his class who annoyed the teacher 'and was hung-up by his braces on the hook on the back of the door'.

An astonished grandchild asked: 'That must have been so sore. Did his teeth break?'

WE asked for your daft Hallowe'en costumes, and a Kirkintilloch reader claimed: 'One year my son dressed our pet dog as a cat. He then complained it wouldn't come when he called it.'

ALSO not perhaps spending a lot of time over their costume was the girl who got all those little glass jars out of her mum's cupboard, put them on a tray she carried in front of her, and told folk opening their doors that she was 'a Spice Girl'.

MEDIA trainer Charles Fletcher was helping a journalism student at Glasgow Clyde College's radio station where he got an interviewee on line, and, before handing her over to the student presenter, asked the customary question all radio stations do to check sound levels: 'What did you have for breakfast?' There was silence on the line, so Charles tried to encourage her: 'You can just make something up if you haven't eaten today,' and eventually the girl blurted out: 'Toast.' Satisfied, Charles handed her over to the presenter who began the interview: 'Thanks for joining us today. Now, eating disorders and your personal experience.'

A STUDENT from Glasgow returning to university in Leeds tells us about the perfidy of mothers. The student explains that before returning north from Leeds for the Christmas holiday, her mother insisted on the phone: 'Bring your laundry with you. I don't mind doing it.'

But after returning home she heard her mother on the phone to a friend: 'Typical student. She walked in the door with a big bag of washing for me to do.'

A GROUP of Glasgow University students put up American computer specialist Edward Snowden, the chap who revealed the US's spying secrets, as a candidate to be the university's next rector. It reminds us of when actor Richard Wilson was elected rector at the yoonie. He tells the story that he was appearing in a play in London at the time, and told the producer he had to go to Glasgow for his rectorial installation.

'Is there not a hospital here in London that can do that for you?' she asked.

A HYNDLAND reader tells us he was trying to round up the family for a trip to the cinema and was concerned about being late when his teenage daughter headed to the loo to put on make-up. As they were going to be sitting in a dark cinema he felt it was not unreasonable to shout at her: 'It's a cinema. Even your mum's not bothering with make-up.'

'She doesn't have to,' shouted back his daughter. He thought she was being complimentary until she added: 'No-one's going to be looking at her.'

A READER tells us he was listing all the ways his life was tougher to his teenage daughter.

He now realises that perhaps it wasn't that bad, as he ended up telling her: 'In my day you had to answer the phone without knowing who it was that was calling.'

ELIZABETH DICKINSON reads on the noticeboard for the Gallery Apartments student accommodation in Glasgow's Port Dundas that it is 'suitable for duel occupancy', and tells us that she never realised it was that difficult to secure student digs.

SHOPPING in a Glasgow south-side supermarket, a reader heard an annoyed mother tell her son: 'Stop picking your nose!' But the little lad replied: 'So why did they make nostrils the same size as fingers?'

YES, the students are finally back at university after the long summer recess. A new student at St Andrews tells us that she knew it had a reputation for posh students, but she was surprised that when she was filling out the university's gym membership, the drop-down window on the website offered Earl, Duke or Baron as a title option after the more mundane Mr and Mrs.

THANK goodness the School of Art has been saved. Former student Deedee Cuddihy was discussing the fire there with a fellow former student who suggested that as many of the college's library books had gone up in flames they should make an appeal for all the students in the sixties and seventies who actually borrowed books without returning them to do so, and the library would soon be restocked.

Added Deedee: 'In some ways it's a wonder that the art school hadn't caught fire before, when you think that back then we were allowed to smoke inside, in amongst all that turps and paint rags. One member of staff in the library smoked so much that there was always a haze hanging in the air. Probably one of the reasons why the wood in the library was so dark. It was the fag smoke.'

COMEDIAN Mark Thomas who headlined the *May Day* show in Glasgow, put on Twitter on the eve of April 1: 'Watched with pride as daughter scraped the filling out of the Oreo biscuits, refilled with toothpaste, and put them back into the packet, ready for tomorrow.'

IF you go into a bar or a restaurant in St Andrews, the chances are the young staff are students. Which explains why, when a reader was in a takeaway, a couple of girls ordered pizzas with extra cheese, and the young man serving them confidently told them: 'Ah but cheese will make you fat, and you won't find a husband then. And that will make me sad for you.'

A READER sends us a link to a website giving the pros and cons of various universities. We are drawn to a comment about St Andrews University. There, an observer of student-life there opines: 'It's dark for ten months of the year, so they all have excellent eyesight. Like badgers.'

TALKING of teenagers, many of them earn a bob or two by babysitting. One girl tells us she heard the two little ones she was babysitting whispering in the bedroom. The older girl was winding up her little sister by saying: 'But what if she's wearing a mask, and she really is the devil babysitting us?'

THE joys of being young. A reader on the train in Clydebank heard a young chap protest to his pals: 'I wasn't that drunk.'
But a pal replied: 'So why did you try to get in through the cat flap when you realised you'd forgotten your key?'

A STIRLING reader received the following text from his teenage son: 'Sometimes I use big words I don't fully understand in an effort to make myself sound more photosynthesis.'

MANY mothers will identify with the thoughts of Scots singer Eddi Reader, who commented: 'Big day today – youngest leaving Scotland just like I did in 1979. Family coming up to mop me up. Mom coming to say, 'See!''

A READER heard a teenager on his bus into Glasgow complain to his pal that he couldn't dance. He was impressed by the advice the pal gave him. 'Can't dance?' he said, 'Just write your name in the air with your bum. Sorted. Next problem?'

MOTHERING Sunday, and a reader tells us he searched in vain for a card that would express the honest view: 'Dear Mum. Thanks for lying to Dad about being on the Pill all those years ago.'

TALKING of youngsters, a Motherwell reader saw that the little boy next door had been given a watch for his birthday, which he was proudly wearing. So our reader says to him: 'What's the time?' The little one looked at his watch and replied: 'It's right now', which our reader couldn't really fault.

STUDYING can prove difficult for students. Natalie Rowley says she was in the library at Edinburgh University when the weather was a bit parky, but nevertheless there was a fellow student sitting there in shorts and a t-shirt. Natalie says: 'It was pouring outside and his friend asked him why he was wearing shorts and flip-flops. He replied, 'I figured if I came in dressed like this, it would make outdoors seem even more cold and then I wouldn't want to leave the library. So this is my way of forcing myself to revise.''

A READER swears to us he heard a teenager on his train into Glasgow tell his pal: 'I had to read George Orwell's *1984* for English. You wouldn't believe how strange the world was back then.'

BEING a bit of a philosopher was the student in Glasgow's west end who told a fellow student: 'The worst part about looking for a job is if you're successful, you end up with a job.'

A GROUP of chaps in a Glasgow pub were reminiscing about their younger days. One of them moaned: 'I used to get upset when my mates were out playing without even asking me along.

'Totally uncalled for.'

OH YES it is panto time, and Kevin Toner was at *Mother Goose* in the south-side's Eastwood Theatre, enjoying the sword fight. Kevin says: 'After several theatrical swings and jabs the goodie disarms the baddie who pleads his innocence and says he'll change his ways. 'Should I let him off?' shouts the goodie. 'Naw!' screams a wee girl aged about five. 'Stab 'im!' 'Surely not a resident of Giffnock or the Mearns . . .'

OUR occasional series of dads who think they are funny. A young woman in Milngavie asked her dad what French toast was and he smilingly told her: 'Just regular toast that smokes cigarettes and has a tiny moustache.'

'You are such a sad man,' she told him.

CHILDREN are growing up so quickly. A reader was stunned when she asked her eight-year-old son what he would like for his birthday, and he replied: 'What's your budget?'

A KILMACOLM pensioner was buying a Sunday newspaper and the newsagent asked him for £2.50 – he really should have gone for the far cheaper *Sunday Herald*. This proved too much for the young chap in the queue behind him who blurted out: 'Two pound fifty for a paper?' He then added: 'Thank God I cannae read.'

JOB interviews continue to be tricky things for young folk after leaving school or university. A reader heard one young girl on the bus tell her pal: 'Then they asked me what my weaknesses are. I told them "Aeros and Yum Yums" but now I'm thinking that's not the answer they were looking for.'

THE universities will soon be back, which reminds a reader of the story about the Glasgow student who attached five £20 notes to his test paper with a note saying 'a pound a mark'. He got the paper back with a mark of only 40, and £60 in change.

GERRY McCULLOCH was in a cafe in Rothesay when an unruly young lad started firing plastic arrows from a toy bow around the café much to the trepidation of the diners.

Finally one of the so-called responsible adults with the urchin shouted: 'Haw Jack! Stop that!' However, Gerry's relief was temporary, as the adult then added: 'Yur no' haudin' it righ'. Here, let me show ye how.'

PARENTING advice in a Glasgow pub at the weekend where a chap was complaining about all the shouting he had to do just to get his family together as everyone seems to be doing their own thing around the house.

'Save your voice,' piped up a chap further down the bar. 'Just turn off your wi-fi router and wait beside it. They'll all be down in seconds.'

16
Office Working

The problem with writing 'The Diary' is colleagues who think they are comedians. This is what we had to put up with – plus some other work stories.

A COLLEAGUE wanders over to tell us: 'We had to toss a coin to decide on the name for our son. Welcome to the world, Tails.'

A READER hears an unusual work confession from a girl on the train into Glasgow the other day. The girl told her pal: 'Have you ever been in the loo at the office when someone in the next cubicle is on their phone claiming to be somewhere else? I always flush the toilet at that point.'

'WATCHED an orange parade last week,' a colleague tells us. 'In Glasgow?' we ask.
  'No, an Essex night-club,' he replied.

OUR mention of disguising company expense accounts reminds Eric Begbie of working in Edinburgh's education department when a college principal tried for three years running to buy a Land Rover for the biology department to go on field trips, but was refused.

Says Eric: 'On the fourth year he requisitioned a 'Bioprobe' which was passed without comment. When the Bioprobe was delivered, it was found to consist of a Land Rover fitted with a microscope and a rack of specimen jars.'

A COLLEAGUE wanders over to tell us the latest about being a father. He reveals: 'My son said he wanted an Action Man for his birthday, but now he tells me he wants a Red Indian. So, I've been trying to put a brave face on it.'

OUR story about expense accounts reminds Allan Boyd in Clarkston: 'There was the chap who started a new sales job and claimed for two shirts and two ties on his first week's expenses. His boss told him to remove them as the company wasn't going to pay for them.

'The next week his boss signed his expenses and said, 'I'm glad to see there's no shirts and ties this week.' 'Ah,' said the sales rep, 'they're there, you just can't see them.''

A COLLEAGUE tells us: 'Worried about burglars when you go on holiday this summer? Simply put all your valuables in an empty *X Factor* box set.'

A GLASGOW reader tells us she was getting all nostalgic the other day when they were removing a row of filing cabinets from her office as so many files are now computerised. It reminded her of when her boss was rummaging in the cabinets and angrily asked her: 'How come the Crawford file is behind the Cooper file?' 'It's alphabetical,' she replied. There was a long silence before her boss walked away muttering 'M, N, O, P . . .' under his breath.

A COLLEAGUE claims: 'I converted my car to an off-road vehicle.' He then added: 'That's what happens when you fail your MOT.'

WE return to job applications, and an HR manager tells us the company had a questionnaire on which was posed the question: 'Sum up your strengths in one word.'

An applicant had written: 'I'm very good at following instructions.'

A COLLEAGUE says: 'It's a nonsense. It's nearly ten months to Pancake Tuesday, yet the shops are already full of flour, eggs and milk.'

BOSSES – always good for a laugh. A Glasgow office worker tells us that his boss was in full patronising tone when he explained what they all had to do, then ended his speech with 'I mean, it's not rocket surgery, is it?'

A COLLEAGUE interrupts us with: 'Lost my favourite spanner at the weekend. I know it seems daft, but it's a tremendous wrench.'

TALKING of the office, a chap in a Glasgow pub had a long drink from his pint before telling the fellow topers: 'Turns out the recurring nightmare I've been having is actually my day job.'

A COLLEAGUE comes over to tell us: 'I saw a sign in a shop window, 'Mosquito nets £10' and I thought, 'I didn't know mosquitoes could play the lottery.'

THE weather improving ever so slightly led to more joggers out on Glasgow's streets, but some of them do go on about their exercise regimes a bit. One such runner, in training for some marathon, was stopped as he entered his office the other day and told by a co-worker: 'Unless you discovered a dead body, I don't want to hear about your early-morning run.'

A COLLEAGUE wanders over to tell us: 'I spent seven very frustrating days repeatedly telling my dog, 'heal!' If it doesn't work soon, I might have to take him to the vet.'

A READER was impressed by the supportive nature of the young man's pal when he overheard a student in Glasgow's west-end announce that he wasn't sure whether he should apply for a place on a BBC training scheme. 'Go for it,' said his pal. 'I've seen lots of ugly folk on the telly these days.'

A COLLEAGUE interrupts us with: 'My friend was involved in a one-night stand that went disastrously wrong. He's been married for seven years now.'

THE trade union May Day celebrations in Glasgow include an exhibition of the cartoons of shipyard painter Bob Starrett, who chronicled the UCS work-in. It was Bob who told the tale of Wee Bunty the shipyard worker and her team who had sneaked in a half-bottle to their work.

When it was finished she asked one of the painters to fill the empty bottle with turps. Wee Bunty carefully replaced the cork, went back to the off licence, innocently explained that it smelled a bit off to her, and when the assistant reeled back from smelling it, he promptly replaced it with a fresh half-bottle.

A COLLEAGUE says: 'I asked my boss if I could leave an hour early. He said, 'Only if you make up the time.' So I told him, "Okay. It's forty-five past fifty-six."'

POSH pronunciations continued. Stephen Duffy tells us he was once at a business meeting where the new boss, an Englishman of impeccable manners and bearing, announced that they were all invited to a strategy session being held in Youfal.

Stephen says: 'Afterwards there was some excitement – where were we going – Greece, Turkey? When the invitation arrived we were rather disappointed and deflated to learn it was Uphall, near Broxburn.'

A COLLEAGUE claims: 'All I got for my birthday last week was a pack of sticky playing cards. I found it really hard to deal with.'

Be Safe

Do not accept rides from solicitors

A READER tells us about his businessman pal who was complaining about the new assistant in his office. He needed a copy of his house key so he handed it to her with a fiver and asked her to get him a copy of it. He returned later in the day to find a photocopy of the key neatly placed on his desk. As she presumably pocketed the fiver we have more than a sneaking admiration for her.

A COLLEAGUE disturbs our train of thought with: 'People say I'm a wanton plagiarist – their words, not mine.'

A CHAP in a Glasgow pub asked the other night: 'Do you ever snore so loud you wake yourself up?' As his pals nodded in agreement he added: 'It happened to me once – worst job interview ever.'

WE ask a colleague how his dance lessons are going. 'Not really progressing with my waltz,' he tells us. 'I feel as if I'm taking two steps forward and one step back.'

A COLLEAGUE was telling his followers on Twitter earlier: 'Thanks to all those who helped me find the English translation of 'mucho'. It means a lot.'

READER John Barrowman tells us about a friend running a clothes shop in Kilmarnock who advertised for a new member of staff. A young woman arrived drinking a can of Coke and finishing off a cigarette. The shop owner told her there was no smoking allowed in the shop, or even outside at the door, and that no cans of juice could be consumed in case it got spilled on the dresses.

The job seeker replied: 'Ah'll no boather. It must be like bein' in the jile in here.'

A COLLEAGUE tells us: 'Tried to buy a bull terrier but nobody would sell me one.'

Inevitably he added: 'You just can't get the staff these days.'

A MILNGAVIE reader tells us she was having some work done in the garden when one of the gardeners knocked on the door and asked if he could use the toilet. As she had just washed the kitchen floor, and seeing the state of his boots, she told him: 'I'll just put some newspapers down.'

'I'd rather use the toilet,' he replied.

A COLLEAGUE wanders over: 'Flattery will get you nowhere. Do you know that when that rumour spread, the Flattery bus company eventually went bust.'

WE have a theory that the maintenance staff are often the funniest people in a building. A reader was interrupted in his work in a Glasgow office by such a chap hammering a sign on to the wall. When he finished, he stood back to admire his work and announced: 'That should stay up till it falls down.'

A COLLEAGUE wanders over and we now regret asking him what he'd been up to. 'I was going to take night classes in self-defence, but decided on mathematics instead.' 'Why?' we asked. 'Decided there's safety in numbers,' he declared before wandering off.

A GLASGOW woman was telling her friends she went to her office night out, and then spent the night with the same beer-bellied balding guy as the previous year. 'I thought you worked from home?' said a pal.

'Exactly,' she replied.

A COLLEAGUE says: 'Do you know that you're fifty times more likely to be mugged in Glasgow than in New York?' He then added: 'But that's because you don't live in New York.'

THE news that a whisky distillery might be built on the banks of the Clyde in Glasgow reminds us of workers at a distillery in Airdrie. When the barrels were delivered down a steep ramp, the workers at the bottom would take turns at adopting a bullfighting pose and then shouting 'Olé!' at the last minute as they jumped aside from the speeding barrels.

Honestly, that's the apex of entertainment in Airdrie.

A COLLEAGUE passing our desk says: 'My wife said she had dug a hole in our garden and filled it with water. I think she meant well.'

A COLLEAGUE feels the need to say: 'Had a blazing row with a waiter in a restaurant and he threw a prawn cocktail at my head. Then he shouted, "That's just for starters".'

ANOTHER colleague says: 'I had to cancel that gym membership I took out in the New Year. Just didn't workout.'

A COLLEAGUE swears to us that he heard a wee wumman tell her pal: 'Me? Lazy? Don't get me started!'

A COLLEAGUE wanders over to interrupt us with: 'I've just held the door open for a circus clown. It was a nice jester.'

ANOTHER says his amateur dramatic society is putting on the *Wizard of Oz*. I asked him what part he was auditioning for. 'Well I daren't play the Lion. And not the Tin Man as my heart's not in it. So, I'm going for the Scarecrow – a no-brainer.'

17
Abroad

Not all our stories originate in Scotland.

AS ithers see us. Foster Evans sends us a copy of the *Chicago Sun-Times* where writer Mona Charen visited the Edinburgh Fringe and reported: 'The Fringe is a festival of performances, and just based on the descriptions available, many of the offerings were repellent.

'This is not to single out the Scots. The leftist tripe and cultural waste they're enjoying is available in every western capital. The difference is that the relentless leftism goes almost entirely unrebutted there.'

We like the reader who added the comment on the newspaper's website: 'I bet you are absolutely no fun at parties.'

WE note on the BBC's news website that their China reporter, Eaglesham's very own Martin Patience, was manhandled by police while trying to report on a dissident's secret trial. We remember when Martin was stationed in Israel and had gone to a hotel to meet a tourist who thought he was Jesus Christ – it's a phenomenon known as Jerusalem Syndrome as people can become mentally imbalanced surrounded by all the religious iconography there.

He was told the chap had left the hotel and, as a disappointed Martin walked away, the helpful receptionist shouted over: 'Wait. We've got a John the Baptist if that's any help.'

AMERICAN sports website *Soccerly* interviewed Partick Thistle's Mexican player Gabriel Piccolo about playing in Scotland – he'd like to wear gloves because it's so cold, but doesn't think it's the right image for a centre-back. Anyway when asked what it was like walking into the Firhill dressing room – they called it locker room – for the first time, he told them: 'I thought they were speaking French or German. I was like 'Are they speaking English, really?' I didn't understand anything in the first two weeks.'

THE TORONTO Globe and Mail newspaper was discussing weather around the world and explained: 'The Scots have particular fun: on a miserable day, you might say it's 'dreich oot', and if a terrible hurricane tears through the country, as one did in 2011, you might take the name it had been given and change it something a wee bit saucier. Thus Friedhelm became Hurricane Bawbag, and the Scots laughed at it even as it ripped the roofs off barns (a word of advice: don't say 'bawbag' to your new Scottish friends).'

NATIONAL GEOGRAPHIC in America sent Andrew Evans to visit Barra and he wrote that he asked a shop assistant at Glasgow Airport if she had ever been there. Continued Andrew: ' "Aye!" she surprised me, "I had my first drink in Barra!" "So it was fun then?" I asked, imagining her among a crowd of young people in a dark pub. "I was eleven years old," she surprised me again. "I was in the pub wi' my family and the folks there jes' handed me a pint." ' Somehow you never see that on the Visit Scotland advertisements.

FORMER Clyde Valley Stompers musician Peter Kerr has just learned that his book about uprooting his family to take over an orange tree farm on Majorca, entitled *Snowball Oranges*, has been translated into Russian because of growing numbers of Russians heading to Spain.

Peter tells us that, on their first Christmas there, the old Majorcan farmer across the road offered to sweep their clogged chimney. Says Peter: 'He arrived with a ladder and a sack containing his chimney-sweeping apparatus, and emptied contents of sack down the chimney.

'There was much noise from up the lum, heaps of soot came tumbling down, followed by the 'apparatus' – a live hen. It worked a treat, and the hen just shook off the soot, clucked indignantly, and wandered back over the lane.'

AMID the glamour of the Golden Globe film awards, you might have missed award-winning Mexican director Alfonso Cuaron thank Sandra Bullock, star in his film *Gravity*, for not taking offence when she misheard his accented voice and thought he had promised her that he would 'give her herpes'. He had in fact told her he would give her an earpiece.

A READER sends us a cutting from the London edition of the listings magazine *Time Out* in which someone claims: 'Being fancied by someone ugly is like winning Scottish Footballer of the Year.'

MUSICIAN Roy Gullane was in Germany where a sandwich shop was obviously keen to publicise it used a lot of sausage and cheese in its fillings. The shop, noted Roy, was called the 'Wurst Käse Scenario'.

A READER in a Sussex bar tells us the Scottish reputation for meanness is even exploited by native Scots. He was in his local where there was a dispute between drinker and barman on whether he had proffered a £10 or a £20 note for his drink. Our reader then heard the toper tell the barman: 'I'm Scottish, so I know exactly how much money I had.'

Faced with this irrefutable logic, the barman immediately gave him the change from a twenty.

RECENT weather has made a few Scots think of buying a holiday home abroad. The story goes of one couple visiting Portugal who were told by the local bar owner of the lovely cottage next to his being up for sale. After they bought it he told them that it needed some work as the roof leaked in the winter and the plumbing was shot to pieces. 'Why didn't you tell us that before?' they asked.

'Weren't neighbours then,' he replied.

WE mentioned that the new pound coin will be twelve-sided like the old thrupeny bit. A reader says: 'No doubt it will mean the reinvention of an old joke that was around at the time of the thrupenny bit. It will now be, 'At least you can use a spanner to get a pound coin out of a Scotsman's hand.'

A READER on the Isle of Man confirms the island perhaps moves at a more sedate pace than mainland Britain. He tells us: 'On one occasion the weatherman on Manx Radio announced, "Here is the weather forecast. Oh, I seem to have forgotten to bring it in, so I'll read out yesterday's instead."'

OUR story about Latin being encouraged again in Scots schools reminds the Rev. Eric Hudson in Bearsden of a couple of educated chaps visiting China who came across a bus stop which had written below the Chinese destination signs, the phrase 'Sub Lapicinum'. Both thought their Latin was quite good, but they were unable to work out what the sign meant. They later discovered that a worker had been sent out to help visitors by painting 'Municipal Bus' at the stop, but wrote it from right to left.

ST PATRICK's DAY, and Duncan Cameron, speaking at the St Paddy's Breakfast at the Indigo Hotel in Glasgow, said he was once told by Irish rugby legend Willie John McBride of a train stopped at Limerick station with the guard walking through the carriages shouting: 'Is there an Irish priest on board?' When he got no response, he was approached by a Presbyterian minister who came out of the first-class carriage and asked if he could be of assistance, fearing it was a matter of life or death.

'I don't know,' said the guard. 'Do you have a bottle opener?'

ANDY SCOTT's awesome Kelpies near Falkirk have been dismissed by a London newspaper's art critic as 'a pile of horse poo'. Among the hordes of angry lovers of the horses' heads who wrote to complain, was one reader who wrote: 'A weegie enters a bar in

Spain where Picasso acolytes are singing the praises of his latest work. "That's pure rubbish" opines the weegie.

'"Senor," says an acolyte, "If you don't apologise, the master will put that smile on the other side of your face."'

WORLD news, and the United States has offered Ukraine a $50 million aid package, provided the country's leader tackles corruption in the country. Our political contact phones to tell us: 'Yes, if anything is likely to stop corruption, it's bribing someone to stop corruption.'

A GLASGOW reader was on a break in Paris when the kindly waiter at the pavement cafe brought out a bowl of water for a panting dog that a local woman sitting at an outdoor table was carrying. When the waiter disappeared the woman threw the water into a plant pot and refilled it with bottled water she took from her bag.

THE Barras continued. Bobby Buirds tells us: 'The wife's cousin was over from Charleston, South Carolina, and visited the Barras a few years ago. She was looking for a flag for her car aerial, and she asked the stall holder, "Have you got a Scottish flag I can put on my antenna?"

'The guy replied, "Mrs – what planet are you from?" The place fell apart.'

IAN McLEAN saw an American couple in Glasgow city centre looking at a poster advertising sightseeing excursions by the company Mercat Tours. 'Arnold, do you want to come and see the meerkats?' one of them asked her partner.

'DID you hear that the King of Spain had abdicated?' said the chap in the Glasgow pub the other night.

'Ah well,' replied a fellow toper. 'Another Juan bites the dust.'

A READER just back from Majorca felt for the father who was pointing out to his toddler son: 'See that dark area in the water slowly moving? It's a lot of fish swimming together.'

As the two of them stood there watching it, the little lad excitedly shouted: 'They're on the sand!' His dad quietly answered: 'Or it could be a cloud.'

AS ithers see us. A reader in America sends us a joke from his local newspaper. By the way, it does actually say 'Hoot', as the typesetter presumably thought 'Hoots' was a mistake.

Anyway, it states: 'A Scotsman, planning a trip to the Holy Land, was aghast when he found it would cost $50 to rent a boat on the Sea of Galilee. 'Hoot mon,' he said, 'in Scotland it wouldna ha' been more than $20.' 'That might be true,' said the travel agent, 'but you have to take into account that is water on which our Lord himself walked.'" "Well, at $50 for a boat," said the Scotsman, "it's no wonder he walked."'

IT'S not just on the Glasgow Subway that people think they are comedians. Nigel Manuel in New York says: 'I was sitting on the subway going into Manhattan last week when an elderly guy with a walking stick slowly limped on board and plopped down beside a well-dressed lady heading to work. 'That's it', he said, 'no more skateboarding for me'. He made my morning, but of course the lady pretended not to hear him.'

A LOT of folk are abroad on holiday just now with their families, taking advantage of the cheaper prices before the English schools break up. A reader on a Mediterranean beach tells us he heard a fellow Scot, a mother, shout out to her bathing children: 'Watch out for thae prisoners of war!' He assumed she had got a bit mixed up about her jellyfish, but he nonetheless had a quick glance over in case some chaps were coming out the water with their hands up.

YES, it's holiday time and a Renfrewshire reader just back from Dingle in Ireland says he was taken with the thoughtfulness of the restaurant owner who asked the last table of diners if they would like to take their desserts at a table out in the garden.

The owner then spoiled the moment by explaining he wanted to get down the local pub before closing time and he wanted to lock up.

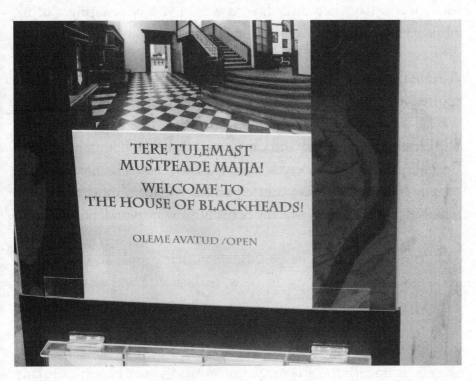

RON BEATON in Dunblane reads in the *Herald* that: 'A Spanish man was gored in the encierro' during the Pamplona bull run, and hopes that the encierro is not in the area below the waist and above the knees.

IT'S that time when folk encounter US tourists. Barrie Crawford was in Majorca where, he says: 'In a gift shop I heard an American guy in his late teens comment, "It's great to be in Spain, I can't wait to try that bull wrestling."'

OUR restaurant story about the owner suggesting a party have their dessert in the garden so he could shut up and get to the pub reminds Angus Macmillan of the classic tale: 'There's the two thirsty cyclists who arrived at an isolated pub in Donegal, and were dismayed when the landlord informed them the pub wouldn't be open for an hour. He suggested they sit on the grass outside as it was a warm day, then added: 'And would you be wanting a drink while you're waiting?"

A READER sees the news agency heading 'Ukrainian President spotted in Balaclava' and thinks: 'So how did they know it was him?'

THE rich south of England can seem a different country at times. Edinburgh writer Ben Verth was in Oxford when he heard a chap passing him in the street remark on his mobile phone: 'Yeah, he's rich. Megabucks. Probably wipes his bum with pheasants' wings.'

18
Royalty

There is still much affection for the Royal Family, but officials can go a bit over the top when royalty appears.

WE asked for stories from royal visits, and George Smith in Clydebank tells us: 'Whenever a royal party arrived at the former Riverside railway station to launch a ship at John Brown's yard, the palings which were visible from the train were painted. The other side of the fence, which was invisible to the guests, was left dirty and unpainted.'

AND Allan Macintyre in Stirling tells us about the newly-crowned Queen's whistle-stop visit to Troon in 1953. 'The locals were pleased to see, at long last, a door fitted to the Gents' toilet on the platform of the railway station, which would conceal the white tiled walls.

'The Queen duly arrived, alighted to spend five minutes greeting the Provost, waved, and hopped back on the train for her next appointment. As the train disappeared, the workmen appeared to remove the door.'

ROYAL visits, continued. Ulla-Brita Carlsen in Ayr tells us that when the Queen went on a royal visit to Denmark in the late fifties, the indicator panel on a lift she had to use was covered up as it would come up with the Danish phrase 'I fart' to indicate that it was 'in motion', which obviously was too indelicate for the Queen.

'Needless to say,' says Ulla-Brita, 'my young son would press every lift button he came near in Denmark.'

WILLIE McKEE tells us: 'Many years ago I was installing six-foot computer cabinets at shipbuilders' Yarrow's flash new design suite on the Clyde, to be opened by Prince Charles. At the last minute the security chief realised I hadn't been security cleared, so he locked me in one of my cabinets.'

ROYAL visits continued. Margaret Brown in Bonnyrigg says: 'Many years ago King Olaf of Norway was on a state visit to Edin-burgh and the local schools were getting the afternoon off to see the procession. My mother worked as a dinner lady, and one of the children told her they were very excited because they were going to see King Half-loaf.'

KENNY GILLIES in Yoker points out: 'When the Queen visited Irvine in 1979, a row of derelict shops in the High Street opposite the town hall were painted specially for her visit. They were demol-ished for redevelopment a couple of weeks later.'

MORE Royal visits. Says Gordon Casely: 'In 1977, Glasgow was first stop on the Queen's Silver Jubilee Tour, and ahead of the royal procession, the streets were to be sanded to give grip to the horses.

'The Queen was due at Glasgow Cathedral, and as the time for the royal appearance drew near, the cheering grew louder, and round the corner came two cleansing department gritters, busy sanding the road, with the boys in the cabs royally waving to the lieges. They almost gained as big a cheer as HM herself.'

THE story about the Queen arriving at Glasgow Cathedral reminds Clare Taylor: 'The reason it got such a cheer was that the driver shouted out 'she's in the back' as he entered Cathedral Square before the Queen's expected arrival.

DAVID CAMPBELL tells us: 'Princess Margaret visited RAF South Cerney and the station was tarted up in the usual fashion, grass cut, stones painted white etc. In addition, a local florist was commissioned to brighten up the borders on the driveway up to the main gate. He duly appeared and planted the blooms, curiously, still in their orange flowerpots. The reason for this became clear for, as soon as HRH had gone, he re-appeared, dug them up and took them away.'

19
Tenement tales

Stories from the Glasgow tenements, and others that just cannot be categorised.

THERE was the tenement blaze in Glasgow many years ago where the fire brigade found a fractured gas pipe. Planning to plug the escaping gas temporarily, the senior officer asked a new firemen to borrow a potato from one of the neighbours.

He came back with a packet of Smash and asked if that would do instead.

OUR request for tenement tales leads to one reader telling us about a couple in Clydebank during the Clydebank Blitz exiting from their top-floor tenement flat to go to the air raid shelter. When they reached the bottom of the stairs, the wife told her husband: 'I'll need to go back up – I've left ma teeth.'

Disabusing her, hubby replied: 'It's bombs they're droppin' – no aipples.'

A READER reminds us of the postie delivering a letter to a west-end student flat in Glasgow. Having climbed to the top floor without finding the name on any of the doors, he was left with the last flat where, due to the transient nature of the students using it, the names of the occupants were written on a sheet of paper.

The postie, reluctant to try anywhere else, took out a pencil, added the name of the person on the envelope, and popped the envelope through the letterbox.

THE tenement stories allow Andy Cameron to tell us: 'We used to play a game in the tenements called CDRA (Chap Door Run Away). Nowadays it's called Parcel Force.'

DONALD MACASKILL in Glasgow tells us about two students in the 1960s who were employed by pollsters to find out the political opinions of folk in a swathe of west-end tenements. The students, who wanted to get back to the pub sooner rather than later, devised a plan that if the flat door had polished brass then the occupant was put down as Tory, polished timber, Liberal, and the new fashion for terrazzo tiles, Labour. Dirty timber had you marked down as undecided.

TENEMENT tales continued. Norman Lawson says: 'We once inherited an upright piano from an old aunt who lived in a four-storey tenement in Glasgow. When I telephoned the removal man, he said, 'It'll be on the top floor.' 'When I asked him how he knew that, the weary response was, "They always are".'

BILL Taylor reminds us of the apocryphal tale: 'There was the Edinburgh lady who moved to a top-floor tenement flat in Glasgow. In spite of the prim face that she presented to neighbours, she had a guilty secret – a 'gentleman caller' – whom she would 'entertain' every week. Imagine her horror when he collapsed and died in her arms.

'Mortally embarrassed at what people would think, she was forced to seek the help of her neighbour across the landing. This resourceful Glasgow lady surveyed the body for a moment and then said, 'Jist put a shammy in his haun, and throw him oot the windae.''

NEWTON Mearns reader Harvey Ockram, driving on the A83, stopped at the Rest And Be Thankful viewpoint, where a lone piper was playing a soulful lament, watched by a quiet yet appreciative audience. When he finished he went into his case and brought out a container. Assuming he was passing it around for donations, Harvey stepped forward, hand outstretched with a pile of coins, only to realise too late that the chap was unscrewing an urn and scattering the ashes of a loved one at the viewpoint.

It was an awkward few moments before Harvey could slip away.

TENEMENT tales continued. Says Morag Jones: 'In the mid-eighties when living in a Bruntsfield tenement in Edinburgh, we had an elderly neighbour in his nineties. He had lived there since a young man, when his employers had told him he could stay for as long as wanted for a nominal rent. He could however only have either a brass nameplate or a letter box on his front door – and yes, being Edinburgh, he chose the name plate.

'He never did have a letter box.'

AND tenement life takes us to stairheid rammies. Sheriff JP Murphy recalls: 'One example involved two doughty ladies who came to blows on the landing and breached the peace to an extent that brought them both before the court. One claimed that the cause of the trouble was the abuse by the other of a new arrival in the close, a young mother. "She called her a clarty besom," she explained. "And, of course," said the fiscal, herself a young woman, "you rushed to deny this slur on your new neighbour."

'"No, it wisnae that," replied the accused. "She is a clarty besom, but that's her ain business."'

JOE McKENZIE at the Griffin Bar in Glasgow, across the road from the King's Theatre, is still scratching his head after two ladies came in the pub after attending the musical *Cats*. As it was early in the evening, he asked them if they had nipped out at the interval, but they informed him they had walked out and weren't going back.

'Why not?' asked Joe. Despite the clue in the title, one of the ladies firmly stated: 'They're all dressed up as cats – and I hate cats.'

A READER on a bus into Glasgow swears he heard a young chap tell his pal: 'I bought the new guy in the office a cup of coffee. But it turns out he wasn't a Secret Millionaire, so it was a complete waste of 80p.'

OUR tenement tales remind David McJimpsey in Cumbernauld of the classic yarn: 'Two older women are leaning out of their tenement windows in the 1960s chatting, when two teenage girls with beehive hairstyles, mini-skirts and high-heels walk past.

'One woman declares, 'look at they two. That's all the young yins think aboot these days – sex. It wasn't like that in oor day. We were too busy hivin weans.'

ANDREW FOGARTY tells us about a slimming club meeting in Paisley where one woman asked another regular where her competitive pal was. 'Running late, as she's doon the toon hall giving blood,' she said.

'She'll do anything to be slimmer of the week,' replied the first lady.

A WHIMSICAL reader phones 'The Diary' to announce: 'Just said 'boo' to a goose. Don't see what all the fuss is about.'

SHOWING that they've been getting away with it for years, Angus Johnston sends us a cartoon by the great Willie Galt in the *Evening Times* in the eighties. It shows a wee Glasgow wifie in a gas showroom and telling the young girl behind the counter: 'Listen hen, ah can remember when gas only went up if ye put a match tae it.'

READERS never realised how educational the BBC was until the BBC Scotland news website told of accidents on an icy Lanarkshire motorway before adding: 'It is believed that ice formed when temperatures fell below freezing.'

'Who said investigative journalism was dead,' says reader Ronnie McLean.

WE mentioned the pantomime season beginning. It is also the time, of course, of hotels putting on Christmas nights out. Barry McGirr at the Leapark Hotel in Grangemouth tells us: 'We've got Liverpool comedian Gary Skyner appearing at our Christmas Dinner Shows this year.

'He was telling the partygoers the other night that he'd been tending his wife's grave in the morning. "She's not aware of that of course," he said. '"She thinks it's a fish pond."'

'I SEE,' says Garscadden reader Michael Bruce, 'that NHS Greater Glasgow's original plan to close the homeopathic hospital has now been watered down. No trace of irony there, appropriately enough.'

AN Ayrshire reader tells us his email account was hacked with some unknown scammer sending out emails to all his friends saying that he was stranded penniless in the Ukraine, and could they send money to get him home. When he discovered what had happened, he emailed his friends to tell them not to send any cash. A number of them assured him that they had in fact sent money to President Putin in return for keeping him there.

HOW do you deal with cold callers on your phone? Gus Furrie in East Kilbride answered one such call and, when the caller asked for Mr Furrie, quickly said he wasn't in. Undeterred, the caller asked who he was speaking to and Gus replied: 'Oh just a burglar who's stealing from the house' and hung up.

Six weeks later he answered the phone and again says to the unknown caller that Mr Furrie wasn't in. 'You must be the burglar then,' said the chap on the phone.

WE asked about daft radio chat and Drew Mackin recalls a chap from Muirkirk telephoning the *Lou Grant Show* on WestSound and being asked by Lou where he was calling from.

'The lobby,' replied the chap.

A TOURIST attraction in Dunblane is the postbox painted gold in memory of Andy Murray's Olympic victory. Local Rob Macken-zie tells us: 'On Monday, a lovely sunny day, I walked to the gold box to post a birthday card to my father. As often is the case, there were a few people queuing to get there picture taken beside it, and as I've done many times, I gave the card to the chap posing so that he could post it to make his picture more authentic.

'This time though the chap looked at the address, and a bit confused, told me, 'This isn't for me!'

BLOKE takes two stuffed dogs onto the *Antiques Roadshow*. The presenter examines them and says: 'Well, this is a very rare set produced by a celebrated company of taxidermists who operated in London at the turn of the last century. Do you have any idea what they would fetch if they were in good condition?' The bloke gives it some thought. 'Sticks?' he asks.

EVER had a rubbish birthday? Jake Lambert passes on to us: 'The night before my friend's seventeenth birthday, his brother borrowed his friend's new car, put a ribbon in it, and parked it in their driveway.'

A PERTHSHIRE reader swears to us that when leaving church on Sunday he heard a fellow worshipper tell the minister as he shook his hand that his sermon hadn't been very good that day. The minister looked shocked, so the parishioner's wife told the minister: 'Just ignore him. He doesn't know what he's talking about. All he does is repeat what he hears other people saying.'

GREAT time of the year to own a dog with all those dry light nights. Many an owner will agree with Amy Vansant who tells us: 'I swear that my dog spends half his time trying to understand what we're saying to him, and the other half trying to pretend he doesn't understand what we're saying to him.'

HARD to believe that not everyone is a dog lover. A reader was walking in Rouken Glen Park when a couple took exception to a dog on an extending lead padding about in front of them, and shouted at the owner: 'Can't you control your dog? It walked right across our path!' Our reader commends the owner's prompt reply: 'What do you expect him to do? Mirror, signal, manoeuvre?'

'DO you know what's fun?' a cyclist phones to tell us. 'Riding one of those bikes with a toddler seat at the back with no-one in it and saying very loudly when you pass folk on the street "You're being very well behaved today".'

A GLASGOW reader hears two women discussing a mutual friend with one of them saying their pal had been on a ballooning holiday. When the second lady expressed surprise, the first one added: 'Aye, she came back three stones heavier than when she went.'

HAVE you noticed some restaurant menus are becoming more Americanised these days? A reader was in one such restaurant where the menu stated your steak came with a choice of a side dish. This must have escaped the notice of the chap at the next table who was asked how he would like his steak cooked.

   After he replied: 'Medium' the waitress asked: 'and which side?' After a certain hesitation, the chap replied: 'Both.'

A WHIMSICAL note from a reader who phones to ask: 'Why do so many pigs die eating an apple?'

A CHAP at a Glasgow golf club told his pals: 'The council has written to me saying that the wheelie bins should be placed at the kerb with the handles towards the street, and the lid closed.

'So I wrote back asking that once they are emptied could they be placed slap bang in the middle of the driveway or two doors down from where I live. And to give them their due, they've followed my instructions to the letter.'

THE NATIONAL Mod had a great week in Paisley. Piero Pieraccini, mine host at the town's Hamishes' Hoose bar, had a large Gaelic banner of welcome to any thirsty attendees. He tells us: 'Leanne, a member of staff, texted me to say that we had been mentioned on the Gaelic television station BBC Alba. I asked her what was said about us, and she replied, 'La da da di la Hamishes' Hoose la di da di la'.

'A bit of work to be done there I think.'

A HOUSEWIFE confesses to us she decided to have some fun with a cold caller who offered a cheaper electricity tariff. She confused the chap mightily by telling him: 'Oh no, I like the electricity we get. I wouldn't want a cheaper version. We don't like buying cheap versions in the Mearns.'

MEANWHILE at the Edinburgh Fringe, the play *Devil in the Deck*, about a smooth-talking grifter, has been criticised by local magicians for revealing how a complex card trick is done. As Paul Nathan from the show magically put it: 'We have run into a bit of controversy from the local magic community. They are grumpy that we reveal how one of our tricks is done. However they are also grumpy because they don't have girlfriends, social skills, or sunshine.'

20
Competitions

Readers enthusiastically embrace 'The Diary' competitions.

WE asked for Scottish TV programmes if the country voted for independence. Some suggestions:

Boggin – the misfortunes of a Danish pastry well past its sell-by date. (Tom Bain).

Strictly Come Chancin – a fly-on-the-wall documentary based at a Glasgow dancehall.

Top Gear – junkies in Scotland's cities comparing the merits of their different suppliers.

The Y Factor – couples wake after drunken seductions and ask the obvious question. (Paul Cochrane).

Mock the Weak – Ian Duncan Smith hosts his hilarious Easter-house-based game show in which contestants try to win a State pittance. (Dave Carson).

Dr Finlay's Facebook – Daily ramblings from an old country practitioner. (Stewart MacKenzie).

I've Been Framed – Reality show televised from Glasgow Sheriff Court. (Ian Barnett).

Come Fine With Me – Trawling the bus lanes of Glasgow with the council's roads department. (Dave Carson).

Braking Bad – Poor drivers caught on camera. (Paul Cochrane).

Who Do You think You are, Pal? – a programme about combative Glaswegians. (Robert Menzies).

Panaroma – an inquiry into the scent of Co-op bread. (Brian Chrystal).

Celebrity Square Sausage – Scottish cookery quiz. (Jim White).

All Craters Great and Small – drama about the state of Glasgow's roads. (Andy Clark).

Weel or No Weel? – Noel Edmonds finds out how a group of Scots are keeping. (Carl Williamson).

Embarrassing Buddies – following St Mirren through a bad spell. (Eric Donegan).

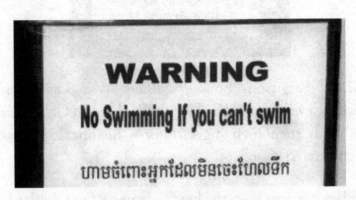

Corporation Street – about Glasgow councillors and their foreign trips.

Sash in the Attic – an ageing Orangeman talking about the old days.

The Ex Factor – tenement dwellers organise their own repairs to save a few bob.

Downtown Cabbie – A Glasgow driver's city centre adventures on a Friday night. (Peter Houston).

Life on Mars – The Glasgow diet explained. (Stephen Gold).

Queue? Aye! – The chat from the toilets at the new Glasgow Hydro. (Jim Gracie).

Game of Throw-ins – Coverage of the less interesting games in Scottish football. (George MacLeod).

Any Persons (Except Players)
Caught Collecting Golf Balls
On This Course Will Be
Prosecuted And Have Their
Balls Removed !

NORMAN Ferguson's book *If History Was Scottish* envisages what historic events would be like if seen through Caledonian eyes. Readers made their own suggestions of historical quotes if they have been uttered by a Scot.

'Remember son, just keep the heid' – James VI to Charles I. (Andy Ewan).

'I'll be home after nine' – Frank Haffey to his family before game at Wembley. (Bill Allan).

'Listen hen, ah'm really no bothered' – Rhett Butler (Allan MacDougall).

'Aye, two single fish an hunners a Mother's Pride should dae it' – Jesus. (Jim White).

'Did you put that chip pan off?' – Mrs Pepys to Samuel. (Andy Gourlay).

'That's a real stoater' – Barnes Wallace. (Carl Williamson).

'Hey Archimedes! The bath's runnin' ower again' – His mother (Carl Williamson).

'So much for Maw telling me to put on clean underpants' – General George Custer (Graham Scott).

'Ta ta the noo' – Captain Oates, the Scott South Pole expedition (Russell Smith).

'Hoy, William of Normandy. Watch it with the arrows. You could take someone's eye out!' (David Walker).

King James IV on the eve of the battle of Flodden: 'Aye, right, you and whit army?' (Jim Black).

'I'll wipe that smile aff yer face, Mona.' – Leonardo Da Vinci (Ian Sharp).

'Oh! Ma heid,' – Sir Isaac Newton.

'Did I hear right, there's free tablet going?' – Moses (George Crawford).

'And if all your friends drove off the pier would you do so, too?' – Ted Kennedy's mother.

21

Sport

If they is one thing Scots love is sport – talking about it rather than taking part, it has to be said.

SCOTTISH Premiership club Hibs announced that it had made a £100,000 profit – the first time it has been in profit for three years. 'That's what happens,' explains our football man in the capital, 'when you don't have to pay any win bonuses.'

WHO could blame England fans for looking forward to the World Cup? An e-mail doing the rounds down south is worth passing on: 'All right mate, are you free in June? You'll never believe it but I've just won an all-expenses paid trip to the World Cup Finals on *Talk Sport*. It's for me and three mates – three weeks all inclusive in Brazil with £2000 spending money. Flights leave from Gatwick, June 10.

'So if you're free, I wondered, could you put my bins out for me?'

POOR start to the season for Manchester United's new Glasgow boss David Moyes. As a Manchester City fan phones to ask us:

'What's the difference between Prince Andrew and Manchester United?' He answers himself: 'Prince Andrew has never regretted getting rid of Fergie.'

FRENCH football club St Etienne is buying the old Hampden football posts for its museum as the club always argued it was the old-fashioned square posts which denied the team the European Cup when they played in the final at Hampden in 1976. It was a memorable final. As my colleague Tom Shields put it: 'I recall the social aftermath when a follower of St Etienne, known as Les Verts, sporting a green and white top hat, was drowning his sorrows, being bought pints and chatting up the girls in a heavy Maurice Chevalier accent. He was, of course, a chancer from Maryhill.'

AN English reader phones after the football the other night to tell us: 'You Scots are taking this independence thing a bit too far. Now you won't even come to the World Cup finals with us.'

THERE was some helpful information from Scottish-based online turf accountant McBookie which told customers: 'England are 20/1 to win the World Cup in Brazil this summer. For those who don't understand odds, that means if you put on £1, you will lose £1.'

THE nights are fair drawing in, which can only mean that the annual dinners of rugby clubs and golf clubs are not far away. A reader tells us of attending one such boisterous gathering at a rugby club where the guest speaker was droning on interminably. One unruly guest could stand it no longer, and threw a bread roll at the speaker, but hit the chairman of the event, who was sitting next to him, squarely on the head. The chairman merely stood up and announced: 'Hit me again – I can still hear him.'

GLASGOW writer Allan Morrison, in his book on Scottish refs, entitled *Should've Gone Tae Specsavers, Ref!*, tells of the St Mirren striker being sent off who asked the referee: 'What for?' 'The rest of the match,' replied the man in black.

COMMISERATIONS to Scots boxer Ricky Burns. who lost his world title to Terence Crawford in a spirited bout at the SECC in Glasgow. There was a lively crowd to see the match, and as one English visitor commented: 'Ricky's the only jock in Scotland fighting on a Saturday night and getting paid for it.'

AYRSHIRE author Ian McMurdo's book, *The Juniors – The Story of Cumnock Juniors Football Club*, includes the tale of Cumnock playing at Lugar where a home player appeared in a pair of grey flannel trousers, tucked into his socks, as he had forgotten his shorts. After he had slid around all over the place, he was told by Cumnock's Jim

'Maxie' McCulloch: 'You'll no be going to the dancing tonight with the state of your trousers.'

'Of course I will – these are your trousers I'm wearing,' he replied.

UNUSUAL pronunciations of Scottish football teams by broadcasters and John Boyle in Ardrossan remembers a radio announcer who seemed to think that Dundee United had moved their park to the more exotic location of 'Tannadeetchie'.

THE Dundee-Hamilton game was called off due to a waterlogged pitch, which sounds like bad news for the Lanarkshire fans who made the trip. But as one Hamilton pensioner told us: 'I was unaware that fifteen minutes into my bus journey from Glasgow the match was called off. On arrival at Dens Park I was met outside the Dundee Supporters' Club by a Dundee fan, and immediately huckled inside to be plied with free beers, sandwiches and sausage rolls before being set merrily on my way back to Glasgow by the next available bus.

'Not bad for a 50p booking fee for my concession bus ticket. And Accies didn't lose!'

THE sports news was that English cricketers Stuart Broad and Matt Prior talked a man out of committing suicide when they came across him on the parapet of a Sydney bridge in the early hours of the morning.

'Apparently,' says a reader who calls, 'they told him about the England Test series, and he realised that there's always folk worse off than yourself.'

WELL done the Scottish curlers. As Bill Webster told pals: 'I used to play curling, but had to give it up on religious grounds – the Bible says 'let him who is without sin cast the first stone'. Our team couldn't get started.'

FOLLOWERS of popular Glasgow junior football side Pollok were delighted, but slightly confused, that their Twitter account pollokfc had an extraordinarily high number of followers in Mexico. But as club vice-president Stuart MacDonald explained: 'Initial excitement at the thought of an overseas fan club was dampened, however, when a learned member of the management committee pointed out that a more rational explanation could be achieved by splitting the Twitter account into two parts, 'pollo' and 'kfc', with pollo being the Spanish word for chicken. Mystery solved.'

WE asked for your racing stories to mark the Cheltenham Festival, and a reader in Ayrshire tells us of a chap in Cumnock who borrowed a few quid from a friend to buy some food for the family. However, the chap who lent the money later bumped into his pal in the local bookies where he was putting on a bet. 'Here you!' said the angry chap. 'I thought you needed the money to go shopping?' 'I did!' his pal protested. 'I've got gambling money – it was money for the food I was short of.'

MURDOCH McGREGOR was at the Alloa Half Marathon when one of the last women to finish dragged herself over the line with the remaining spectators cheering her like a champion. Murdoch wondered why her t-shirt had 'I was a potato' printed on the front until she staggered past and he read on the back 'But I've got off the couch'.

ON the question of World Cup commentators, Irish bookies Paddy Power summed up what many people think of ITV presenter Adrian Chiles when it tweeted: 'Adrian Chiles could be giving directions out of a burning building and I still think I'd tell him to shut up.'

WEST End football club Broomhill has been given entry to the Lowland League, and could be promoted the following year to the professional leagues, even though they don't actually have a football ground. Instead the Broomhill lads will be travelling to the more challenging area of Possil to ground-share with Ashfield Juniors at Saracen Park. 'The locals,' says one junior football observer, 'will be puzzled by the delay to the kick-off as all the trendy west enders visiting for the first time will want to feng shui the park before the game.'

RUGBY ref Ed Crozier was in charge of a charity game at Cartha Queens Park to raise funds for the Prince and Princess of Wales Hospice in Glasgow. With the players not being in the first flush of youth by many a decade, former West of Scotland captain John Lonergan looked at the approaching rainclouds and told Ed: 'That'll frighten the Kiwi.'

Ed replied that he didn't know there were any New Zealanders playing that day, but John merely nodded towards a fellow player with a suspiciously dark head of hair for his age and said: 'No, the Kiwi polish that'll run down from his hair if it gets wet.'

WE wish Celtic legend Danny McGrain all the best after he suffered a mild heart attack. Friend and former colleague Chick Young, normally a sports reporter, of course, was once hired to MC the opening of a housing development by Australian chanteuse Dannii Minogue. Chick couldn't overcome his years of experience and instead boomed out over the microphone as the elfin-like singer climbed onto the podium: 'Ladies and gentlemen, put your hands together and give a warm welcome to Danny McGrain!'

A CELTIC fan tells us he was en route to the game on Saturday, and feeling a bit peckish he stopped at a burger van for some sustenance. In front of him a rather bulky chap asked for two cheeseburgers, and perhaps feeling he was being judged by the server, he added: 'One's for a pal.'

As he walked away with his fare, the woman who served him

muttered: 'Pal my backside.' And she may not have actually said backside.

'THE bank phoned me because of suspicious activity on my credit card,' said the chap in the Glasgow pub the other night.

'They couldn't believe I'd joined a gym.'

WE thought jokes about football boss David Moyes would have ended since his exit from the Manchester United job. But a final one from a reader down south who tells us: 'I hear that the right wing Ukip party is trying to sign up Moyes to be a party official – they're very impressed how quickly he was able to get united out of Europe.'

IAIN MACDONALD in Oban passes on: 'ITV's Clive Tildsley's gem of information during the Argentina v Iran game on Saturday was inspired. He told us that instead of the usual practice, 'A lot of the Iran players have their Christian names on the back of their shirt'.'

WE mentioned World Cup commentators, and Alastair McKenzie in Bearsden tells us: 'I enjoyed this classic from the commentator after the French had scored yet another goal against the Swiss.'And now, not for the first time, there really is a huge mountain between France and Switzerland.'

WELL ok, just a final one about England as we won't be able to mention them again. 'I don't really know my best position. Left, right or centre.'

'Wayne, just get on the plane and pick a seat, will you?'

SLOWLY the football season is getting under way. Reader David McVey was at a pre-season friendly when, with twenty minutes to go, nine substitutions were made all at once. 'That's not substitutions,' remarked the fan in front of David. 'that's a pitch invasion.'

SEEING Walter Smith at an awards ceremony reminds us of when Walter left Rangers as manager and soon after was in the Ben Nevis bar in Finnieston with protege Ally McCoist having a quiet pint. Landlady Elaine Scott went into the kitchen to fetch some food for other customers and allowed Walter to go behind the bar to pour his own pint. At that another customer walked in, stopped dead at seeing Walter at the taps and asked: 'Is he working here now?'

A READER at a Dollar Academy dinner was much taken with guest speaker Iain Milne, the former international rugby player, explaining that he was capped forty-four times for Scotland. His brother Kenny was capped thirty-nine times for his country. Their brother David managed only one cap for Scotland.

'Or as he likes to tell people,' explained Iain, 'he's one of the three Milne brothers who between them have played eighty-four times for Scotland.'

DAVID LEGGAT's book *Struth*, the story of legendary Rangers manager Bill Struth, reveals that a young Bill was a professional runner. Having arrived in Wales for a race, he didn't have enough money for the train fare home and was appalled to see the handicapper had given him an impossible task.

Thinking on his feet, Bill pretended to be a spectator, then joined the race twenty yards further forward, and secured victory. Before the starter could react, Bill grabbed his winning voucher, galloped to the bank to cash it, then ran to catch the first train out before he was stopped. Years later he sent the race meeting a donation amounting to ten times that of the prize money.

DUTCHMAN Louis van Gaal has been appointed manager of Manchester United. A reader down south heard a chap in his local ask: 'Do you think his English is good enough to be understood by the players?' 'A lot better than the last two managers,' replied a fellow toper.

CLYDEBANK stand-up Kevin Bridges, watching the referee in the Belgium versus Algeria match use the new spray foam to mark ten yards back from the ball at a free kick, told his fans: 'This ref's not holding back spraying that foam – you wouldn't want to fall asleep at a party in his house.'

ONE of the joys for youngsters at the World Cup is collecting the stickers for their World Cup album. An Edinburgh reader heard a young lad say to his bag-laden mum: 'Can I have a packet of stickers?' His exasperated mum held up the bags she was carrying and told him: 'No, you've had a lot bought for you already today.'

'So why not finish the job?' tried the young lad.

CHARITY auctioneer Willie Paterson, raising money for leading Scottish children's charity Aberlour at a dinner in Glasgow, was seeking bids for a football shirt signed by young *One Direction* singer Louis Tomlinson. Willie shocked the charity's guests by announcing that boy band star Louis was 'good in bed'.

He then explained: 'Yes, he can now go to sleep at night without having to have a story read to him.'

GUEST speaker at the Aberlour dinner was Olympic gold medal winner, rower Katherine Grainger, who is originally from Bearsden. All the British medallists were invited to Buckingham Palace after the Olympics where Katherine congratulated the Queen on her impressive part in the opening ceremony in the James Bond sketch.

'Oh yes, a few people have been commenting on that,' replied the Queen before her face broke into a huge smile and she added: 'But did you see how well my corgis acted!'

LEITH author Irvine Welsh of *Trainspotting* fame has been on a tour in Switzerland, France, Spain, New Zealand and Australia to promote his latest novel. Staggering off his flight from Australia, Irvine tweeted his fans: 'Been so disorientated on my travels, I even had a bizarre dream that Hibs were relegated!' Nice try, Irvine. Meanwhile a reader phones to tell us that Irvine's fellow Hibs fans, *The Proclaimers*, are having to re-write one of their songs in the light of Hibernian's plight. It will now be: 'Celtic no more. Aberdeen no more. Motherwell no more.'

GREAT game of football between Scotland and Nigeria. Reader William Sharp says: 'I understand that after the match, instead of the traditional swopping of jerseys, the Nigerian team suggested that the players should swap bank details and phone numbers so that the Scotland players could keep in touch.'

CELTIC fans are still trying to work out what to make of their club's relatively unknown new manager Ronny Deila. As a West Ham fan down south joked: 'My mate said to me that he had just heard that Ronny Deila was Celtic's new manager. Looking bemused, I said to him, 'Who?' 'He replied, 'Celtic, a football team from Scotland'.'

SO Celtic manager Neil Lennon has departed. As one fan contacted the club yesterday to say: 'Can I get a refund on the seven months left on the Neil Lennon calendar you sold me?'

JACK HALLEY tells us of his favourite headline from the Saturday sports editions in Glasgow – the pink one or the green one, he's not sure – about a rare St Mirren win at Ibrox on a day of miserable rain. The headline was 'Smirren Reign at Ibrox'.

READER Andrew Gray receives an e-mail from St Mirren Football Club about season ticket prices for next year, and in making a point about the value of the season ticket, the email states: 'Supporters could potentially miss five matches and be no worse off.' Only St Mirren, reckons Andrew, could make not turning up for the matches sound like a good idea.

GREAT scenes in Aberdeen where thousands turned up to see the city's football club parade the League Cup through the streets. A Celtic fan in Glasgow came up with the biting backhanded compliment while watching the scenes on his local's telly: 'Some turn out frae the Aberdeen fans . . . imagine the turnout if they'd won something decent.'

WE mentioned that Fergus McCann, currently being lauded as the saviour of Celtic, could be a tad grumpy at times. A reader tells us: 'Fergus was known by taxi drivers by just four letters when he was in Glasgow – DTJD. He was so fed up at getting advice from the guy in the front of the cab, that he'd get in and mutter, 'Don't talk, just drive.''

WE also recall Billy Connolly being invited to the club, and as he was about to be introduced to Fergus, someone whispered to Billy that Fergus was a bit of a stickler about attire, and Billy should really have been wearing a tie.

Billy strode forward, shook Fergus's hand and told him: 'What kind of club is this you're running? I've only been here twenty minutes, and already someone's nicked my tie!'

SCOTLAND'S guilty pleasure – quite a few of us have been getting up early to watch the Olympic curling. One reader recalls: 'It reminds me of when I worked in a large Glasgow hospital kitchen. On a Sunday afternoon when we were on our break we used to play frozen chicken curling down one of the long hospital kitchen corridors.

'Great fun. Just a word of warning – never have chicken in hospital.' We of course point out that this was years ago and that hygiene in Glasgow hospitals is now second to none.

OUR tale of Scottish football fans chanting their invective reminds Kenneth Morin in Newton Mearns: 'I took my wife to her first and only football match at Hampden in the early 1970s, where the crowd were giving it laldy on a chant questioning England captain Bobby Moore's sexuality. 'Which one is Bobby Moore?' she asked. 'none,' I replied. The game was Scotland v Wales.'

'HAVE you been watching any curling?' asked a chap of his pal on a train into Glasgow this week.

'I have,' remarked his mate, who then went for the line: 'But the hairdresser came out and told me to move away from the window as it was disturbing her customers.'

PAUL HARTLEY being appointed Dundee manager reminds an east-coast reader of when Aberdeen were looking for a manager and a number of names were being touted. 'He was a manager of the month' argued one fan, backing his favourite. 'Only when he worked at McDonald's,' was the terse reply from his mate.

ROBERT GARDNER shares with us a recent Radio 4 programme on the rising cost of football where tickets can cost as much as £100. Says Robert: 'An older chap said he could recall many years ago arriving at the turnstile at West Ham United to be told, 'That will be £10 mate'. 'What?', the old chap said, 'I could get a woman for that'. 'The guy on the turnstile said: 'Not for forty-five minutes each way you wouldn't – and a brass band in the interval'.

THE football news down south is the transfer of Spurs player Gareth Bale to Real Madrid for truckloads of money. As one football observer opined: 'If I was spending £90m for something that dives, it better be a submarine!'

FAREWELL England from Brazil, and Robert White ruminates: 'England's sharp exit allowed our neighbours a wee glimpse into what it is like to be Scottish by experiencing the same World Cup woes we used to endure.'